IFE, CRADLE OF THE YORUBA

Mr. J. A. Ademakinwa
The Author

IFE, CRADLE OF THE YORUBA

A Handbook

on

The History of the Origin of the Yorubas

J.A. ADEMAKINWA

Original Foreword by

S.O. BIOBAKU, M.A. PH.D
Former Director, Yoruba Research Scheme,
Ibadan, Western Nigeria

With New Foreword by

TOYIN FALOLA
University Distinguished Teaching Professor
Jacob and Frances Sanger Mossiker
Chair in the Humanities
The University of Texas at Austin

AMVPS

Published by

AMV Publishing Services

P.O. Box 661
Princeton, NJ 08542-0661
Tel: 609-785-5135 Fax: 609-7164770
emails: publisher@amvpublishingservices.com &
customerservice@amvpublishingservices.com
worldwide web. www.amvpublishingservices.com

Ife, Cradle of the Yoruba A Handbook on the History of the Origin
of the Yorubas Parts I and II (originally published in 1958)
Copyright © 2014 The Estate of the late J.A. Ademakinwa/Gbenga
Olayomi

Book & Cover Design: AMVPS Origination & Design Division

Library of Congress Control Number: 2013910162

ISBN: 978-0-9766941-9-9 (PB)

CONTENTS

PUBLISHER'S NOTE

The republication of *Ife, Cradle of the Yoruba A Handbook on the Origins of the Yorubas* was sponsored by the Estate of the late author, Mr. J.A. Ademakinwa. The book has been reissued in a virtual verbatim form with minimal revisions and edits to the original texts in order to preserve the historicity of the author's original work published some fifty-five years ago in 1958. This new edition combines the two parts of the original booklets into one volume and is more or less a replication of the original writings of the author. The minimal revisions made to the text are generally in the area of punctuation i.e. the reduction of the excessive use of hyphens by the author in the texts, a feature of "Nigerian" English writing styles during the early to mid-20th century. In addition, a brief index of keywords has been put in place in the new edition. These revisions were with a view to making the reissued book user-friendly for a new generation of readers.

The other substantial addition to the texts is the new foreword. The late Prof. Saburi Biobaku, a renowned Nigerian historian of his time had written the original foreword to Part I of the original two booklets. In keeping with this tradition, Prof. Toyin Falola, currently one of the most respected authorities on African history and a prolific author was approached to write a new foreword which he so graciously accepted to do. AMVPS, the Publishers of the new edition and the Estate of the late author express their deep gratitude to Prof. Falola for his support of the reissuance of the book. The hope as noted in Prof. Falola's new foreword is that the republication will serve to enlighten a new generation of readers about the origins, mythologies and traditions of the Yorubas, one of the largest and most vibrant ethnic groups of the African continent.

NEW FOREWORD

When this book made its first appearance in 1958, it was well received by lovers of Yoruba history and culture. Indeed, the most famous scholar of the Yoruba at that time, Professor S. O. Biobaku, who encouraged the project, supplied a foreword to the first edition. The reason for reprinting this book is exactly the same reason expressed many years ago: a new generation remains ignorant of the history of their people.

The central focus is the city of Ile-Ife; the author, the late J. A. Ademakinwa, was an Ife indigene. He puts the mythologies and traditions of his people to good use to speak to a host of subjects.

The initial chapters cover the early history and the various origin stories. In them, he dispels the idea of a people without an origin. His work was very ambitious, seeking to trace the origins of names and even some dates associated with early traditions. It displeased him that Ile-Ife had been maligned because many scholars and others did not recognize its status as the cradle of Yoruba civilization. He took the position that the *Ooni* (king) of Ife was not occupying a priestly status and was subordinated to the *Alaafin* of Oyo.

Part One of the book intertwines the history of Ife— "the city of creation"— with that of the entire Yoruba people. He presents the *Ooni* in mythical proportions, and he explains the meanings of words and labels that have stayed with us for so long, such as *Omoluwabi* and Oodua. As common for the time, stories of migrations were fairly widespread, and our able author talks about Egypt and other ancient civilizations. Ademakinwa also explains the origins of practices such as facial marks, slavery, words, and burial ceremonies that he considers deeply rooted and, in some ways, connected with Egypt.

There is so much knowledge to cherish in this section of the book. Indeed, many of the practices that he describes are no more. One example is how people made stone images of themselves (*didi ota*) to confer the status of immortality. Carvings were important, as well as iron casting, and he carefully presents this as evidence of a great civilization.

He reviews the group name of "Yoruba" and suggests that calling the people "Ife" would have been more appropriate. The name "Yoruba," as the author extensively explains, has three origins: as a "despiteful" one to characterize some Oyo people in conflict situation; as a way Christian missionaries recognized their converts; and as a device that assisted British efforts to mark their acquired colony.

Part One includes much material on the nineteenth century, especially on the histories of Oyo, Ibadan, and Modakeke. As the story moves into the twentieth century, he supplies a lot of information to support his assertion that the *Ooni* was the most superior of Yoruba kings.

Part Two of the book covers the history of Ile-Ife in more depth, moving away from the general history of the Yoruba presented in Part One. His intention is to let as many people as possible know about Ile-Ife, its location, its place in Yoruba history, and its significance to human history. The Yoruba were "born and bred" at Ife, which is his way of stressing that they did not come from Egypt. He sees a number of similarities between Ife names and those in the

Bible. Oduduwa, the founder of Ile-Ife, had no father or mother. There are rich mythologies covering so many aspects: creation, leadership, kingship, names, and divinities. He mentions important personalities, as well as festivals and religious celebrations.

This book is a powerful collection of mythologies. It explains how the Yoruba came into being and it puts Ile-Ife at the very center. It includes many major stories on aspects of Yoruba culture. Some of these stories can be treated as "sacred beliefs" as in those of Oduduwa. Myths express politics and political ideologies, and two stand out very clearly in this book: Ife as the cradle of the Yoruba people and the *Ooni* as the preeminent king.

Unlike academic history books, one should not read this book as a series of arguments or as Ademakinwa using data to rethink existing arguments. Books based on myths do not work in this manner. Ademakinwa is trying to portray a specific narrative based on his own background and experience. His accounts, based on mythologies, are regarded as sacrosanct, as the "truth of history." In this definition of history, proverbs, wise sayings, allegories, and the like are all ways to reach the truth, to explain, and to educate.

Ademakinwa displayed his knowledge of the history of other lands, and he linked those historical narratives with the legends of his own people. At other times, he disagreed with those narratives. For example, the early history of England reveals commonalities of explanations. Ademakinwa's book fulfills the goals set out by the author, conveying ideas to understand historical events within the idioms and conception of history by his own people. It links rituals with mythologies to explain events and phenomena. It explains the formation of Yoruba customs and culture in combination with traditional accounts that tell us about Yoruba history and culture. The book deals primarily with a past that is no more, that very distant time not covered by scientific explanations but by mythologies. In this sense, the myths are valid within the rubric of traditional stories.

The book can be enjoyed at multiple levels: as the history of Ife and the Yoruba; as a body of impressive myths about the past; and as the memory of a different age.

Toyin Falola
University Distinguished Teaching Professor
Jacob and Frances Sanger Mossiker Chair in the
Humanities
The University of Texas at Austin

ORIGINAL FOREWORD

I welcome the opportunity of writing a "Foreword" to Mr. Ademakinwa's work, entitled "Ife, Cradle of the Yoruba." A history of Ife or a history of the Yoruba with Ife as its centre piece has been long overdue; the appearance of this book is therefore significant and through it Mr Ademakinwa has made a notable contribution to the study of Yoruba history. With his amazing knowledge of Yoruba traditional accounts and his interest in English history, Mr. Ademakinwa has given us the first two parts of a major work in the present volume which is at once stimulating and authoritative in tradition.

As the public are aware, there is a Yoruba Historical Research Scheme which aims to establish an authoritative version of The History of the Yoruba by employing all modern techniques of delving into the history of non-literate peoples. Mr. Ademakinwa is a valued Research Associate on the Scheme. It is my belief that the first step is to record the traditional accounts, the history of the Yoruba as the people themselves knew it and then trained historians can analyze them and fashion historical material out of them. We are fortunate that we now have a record of the Ife traditions as compiled and digested by a worthy son of Ife. I, therefore, whole-heartedly recommend this work to all those who are interested in Yoruba history and it is my hope that it will have the wide audience which it deserves.

S.O. BIOBAKU
Director, Yoruba Historical Research Scheme

PREFACE

That the origin of the Yoruba has long been enshrouded in profound obscurity is an all truism, frankly acknowledged by all scholars, irrespective of colour, creed or race.

I am fully aware that there have been on the world markets, several books written by eminent persons on the waves of the migration of the Yorubas from one or the other of the Eastern countries like Mecca, Nubia, Egypt and Sudan, partially under the leadership of Oodua (now) generally called Oduduwa, and partly under the hegemony of other unidentified personalities to either Ile-Ife, or some other really unknown parts of our vast country, before dispersing to the various parts of what is known today as Yoruba country.

Nevertheless, finding these theories practically insufficient to solve the agitating problem confronting the entire world in so far as the actual origin of the Yorubas is concerned, both nationally minded individuals and the Western Regional Government of Nigeria have recently made it their incumbent duty to dig deep into the very foundation of the History of the Yorubas with a stout view to knowing their factual origin in order to allay our common bug of being perpetually regarded as "A nation without origin."

As a result of such laborious and painstaking efforts, this book entitled, "Ife, Cradle of the Yoruba," divided into approximately four parts, has been written to fill, to a reasonable extent, the much earnestly needed gap.

In the first two parts of it, which will simultaneously come out very soon, I have endeavoured to bring out as

17

vividly as possible the following, including many other very informative points:

1. The original common name of the people now called Yorubas.
2. Why, many years ago, some of them were known as "Aku" in Sierra Leone; as "Inago" in Lagos, and "Egbas" at Abeokuta.
3. When Yoruba was born and used for a section of us, and later for us all as a national name.
4. Ancient and Modern Yoruba countries and the extent of each.
5. Those who gave us all the name, when and why?
6. From where Oodua (now) generally called – "Oduduwa" and his people came to Ile-Ife.
7. The real people they met there.
8. Origin and the destruction of the Igbos, whom many writers believe to be the predecessors of the Ifes to Ile-Ife.
9. Where the rest of them are yet to be seen today.

What I have laconically enumerated may be regarded as nothing short of only a fractional part of what are actually to be found in these first two parts of the book. Therefore, in offering them to the general public, I should be ungenerous if I did not make full acknowledgement of the material taken as quotations from the following books:

1. *A History for Nigerian Schools (Standard V Pupils Book)*;
2. *Iwe Kika Ekerin Li Ede Yoruba*;
3. *Iwe Kika Ekarun Li Ede Yoruba,*
4. Johnson's *The History of the Yorubas,*
5. *Nigerian Story told for Children* by C.R. Niven.
6. *The Peoples of Southern Nigeria* by P. Amaury Talbot.

Before the final analysis of this "PREFACE" is genuinely made I must show my sincere pleasure in expressing my due thanks to Mr C.J. Lloyd, University College, Ibadan, for his rousing letter and fraternal piece of advice to me in 1952, on the necessity for Ife history, written by an Ife, if really, good progress was envisaged for that ancient city.

In preparing the manuscript of these books for the press, I have had great assistance from Dr. S.O. Biobaku, M.A., PH.D., Director of the Yoruba Historical Research Scheme, University College, Ibadan, to whom I am pleased to avail myself of this opportunity of expressing my warm gratitude.

The suggestion of the appropriate title for the whole of these books has been the laborious task of Dr. Biobaku. On the other hand, the alacrity with which I accepted his fraternal piece of advice and suggestion to perform this laborious duty are the measures of my hearty thanks to him for having so satisfactorily accomplished it.

J.A. Ademakinwa
Retired Schoolmaster

SIR ADESOJI ADEREMI,
K.B.E., C.M.G.
The incumbent Ooni of Ife, and the
Chairman of the House of Chiefs in
the Western Region of Nigeria at the
time this handbook was originally
published. He began his reign on
2nd September, 1930

INTRODUCTION

Throughout the world, it is an undeniable common knowledge that the source of a river is never as wide and deep as any other part of it in its long or short course; and yet, the honour of being the start of a river has never been known to be taken away from any river however tiny it may be.

In ancient times, only a very few extensively travelled elephant hunters were privileged to know the sources of some rivers or streams by mistakes. The opportunity of knowing the sources, courses and mouths of rivers came to us of recent times, through the geographical knowledge which the Western civilization brought to us by our being under the British flag.

Of all the towns of the immensely large country called Yoruba-country today, the small town of Ile-Ife can favourably be compared to nothing short of a big and extensive river, flowing pass through many important places of interest. In the second place, Ile-Ife may prudently be compared to a robust, well-fed and well-to-do mother, who had so many children that in the end, through caring for, and nursing those children earnestly both day and night, she became so sick and emaciated that, not only the outside people, but even her own children were not willing that people should know her as their mother again.

Today, thousands of people do not know that Ile-Ife, which has not even a province of her own as the other towns, once had a mighty empire under the sole kingship of the Ooni of Ife. Notwithstanding, the past written records of the ancient glory of Ile-Ife as a mighty empire are many, but a few of them will be brought out here to support the authenticity of this history.

In the *Iwe Kika Ekarun Li Ede Yoruba* page 85, a part of paragraph 6, it is seen the following: "Ife is a tribe between Ibadan and Ilesha. It is regarded as the cradle, and a place of special honour for all the other tribes of the Yoruba country."

Page 90, paragraphs 1-3 of the same book reads thus: "Historians said that very many years ago, there was at Ile-Ife a man whose name was Lagelu, Oro-Apata-Maja. A great man was he at Ile-Ife; he had a well recognized chieftaincy, and was very brave. His chieftaincy was so important that it could be unhesitatingly called the Balogun title of the present day.

"One fine morning, Lagelu was suddenly seen getting ready with his children, wives, and several of his relatives to leave the town, saying that he was going to carve for himself a town. This kind of attempt was then not a new one; and it was never once related that such a practice did at any time evoke Ooni, the King of Ile-Ife's annoyance. His attitude gave immense privileges to many valiants, who likewise left the town to found other towns in several other places, and became Bales (*not actual kings then*) of their towns; nevertheless, they never failed to acknowledge the suzerainty of the Ooni as their King (*not as a high priest as some people wrongly call him now*). Without much ado, this was what brought about that saying: 'Ile-Ife is the cradle of the whole Yoruba race as well as that of the whole universe.'

"The town which Lagelu founded after leaving Ile-Ife as previously stated is called Ibadan today."

History tells us further that after the evacuation of the

first Ibadan by its inhabitants, on account of an Egungun, whose disguising dress was unexpectedly torn off in the presence of a bevy of women, Lagelu came back to rebuild the town. Equally so are there other records, which show that, the foundation of the third and present Ibadan was not without the Ifes, headed by Chief Shingbusin, whose place, as the head of all the confederate armies of Ifes and Ijebus, Maye, the generalissimo of the Ifes took, after the former went home to report the complete fall of Owu at the hands of the Ifes and the Ijebus to the Ooni.

History will soon show that Ife, as a mother of many sturdy and well-fed children from her maternal breast, once had a massive empire, over which the Ooni ruled as a sole monarch, far from the interior to the coast. That it was through the far-reaching effects of his ancient importance that the Christianity which the Portuguese met at Benin City in 1485, first came to Ile-Ife by way of Abyssinia, before it reached Benin City, will also be shown.

It will also be shown in history that, as a consequence of the potentiality of the position of the Ooni, whom other tribes like the Benis, used to call Oghene, or Ogane then, the name of "Guinea-Coast", with which many of us are familiar today, was derived from his title "Ogane". Vide (*Nigerian Story told for Children* by C.R. Niven, page 48, paragraph 1).

It was the importance of Ogane, whom the Portuguese called Prester John, a mighty African Christian Potentate, that attracted them to the West Coast of Africa, through which they had the Privilege of visiting Benin City in 1485-6.

That Ile-Ife as a frail, and emaciated mother was eventually set aside by both the outsiders and her own children when, owing to the inability of the Ifes to manage their former large empire effectively, coupled with the

23

cunning attitude of the other tribes around them, will be revealed below.

In the proceedings of the Church Missionary Society for the year 1900-1901, page 83, and a portion of page 84, we read the following – "On Easter Day, 1900, he (Rev. R.S. Oyebode), baptized twenty-one persons, the largest number at any one time since he was placed at this station."

Next to this, we read the following – "At Modakeke, there were eighteen baptisms. The adherents number eighty-six and are building a place of worship.

Although Ile-Ife was not mentioned in the above referred to report, yet the eighteen people baptized as well as the eighty-six adherents, building a place of worship were both Ife and Modakeke peoples.

In the paper read by the Rev. (afterwards) Bishop James Johnson in the Conference of the Anglican clergymen, held in Lagos in the month of February, 1896, Ile-Ife was definitely described as a district of Ilesa.

It will now be seen that the sum total of these things was responsible for why anybody going to Ile-Ife towards the end of the last century, and during the very early part of the present century would not like to say that he or she was going to Ile-Ife, but to Modakeke. In addition, the Ibadans and the Modakekes did not consider it an offence to call the Ifes their subject tribe; whereas the Ifes were their quondam benefactors both at Ibadan and Ile-Ife. This was why Ile-Ife was not rightly known to both State and the Church until after the evacuation of Modakeke on the 27th of March, 1909.

Consequently, the situation was so grave that Ooni was no longer known as the original accredited head and father of the Ife race, now called Yoruba race, until the dispute between Akarigbo and Elepe, both of Shagamu in Ijebu-Remo, compelled His Excellency, Sir William Macgregor, the then Governor of Lagos, to invite the late

Alayeluwa, Adelekan, commonly known as Olubuse, the then Ooni of Ife to Lagos in the month of February, 1903.

After all other likely possible means of setting the dispute gravely agitating the minds of both the fighting parties and the Governor himself had entirely proved abortive, the Governor was positively told by those who knew much about the true history of our country that, if he wanted the anxious situation to be eased, he should approach the Ooni of Ife, who, according to ancient law and custom has the last say in such a matter, being the father and head of all the Obas of our land from time immemorial.

Though before that time, the Governor had scarcely heard or known anything about the Ooni, yet he agreed to invite him to Lagos. At first, Ooni declined the invitation, on the grounds that no other Oba of our land had the right of seeing him face to face, and if he was out of his town for some days together, something dreadful would happen in the whole county. The Governor asked whether anything could be done to avert any mishap hat was likely to follow leaving his town for Lagos. After every necessary thing had been done, Ooni agreed to come and honour the Governor's invitation.

When Ooni reached Lagos, he was lodged in a house very near to the late Dr. Henry Carr's house at Tinubu Square. A copy of the photograph he took at that time in Lagos is yet available today.

The quick and wonderful way in which Ooni settled the long standing and previously deep-rooted dispute, and the ready and cheerful manner with which both Akarigbo and Elepe accepted his paternal and impartial decision were so appalling to His Excellency that he immediately promised to visit the Ooni in his very capital town. His Excellency's visit, according to his promise was attested to by Dr. O. Johnson on page 647, of *The History of the*

Yorubas, a part of paragraph 2, reading thus – "Sir William Macgregor, during his regime as Governor, among other places visited Ile-Ife. He granted the Ooni an unusual subsidy on account of his position."

Notwithstanding all the precautions taken against Ooni's going to Lagos with a view to averting the likely attendant evils, the destruction of corn and banana fields of 1903 and 1904 by clouds of locusts and certain insects called 'Topi', so called from their manner of jumping from one place to another, were in many places ascribed to Ooni's visits to Lagos and Ibadan respectively in those two years.

This is a vivid and graphic description of the ancient glory of Ile-Ife, and its extensive empire, which the people, called Yorubas today allowed to decline, by their unfaithfulness to the definite instructions which their progenitor, Oodua gave to their forefathers at the Ita-Ajoro Valedictory Conference of his children with him.

The Oyo and the Benin subsequent empires were mere offsprings of that of Ile-Ife. Therefore, it is wrong history to believe that Alaafin of Oyo was once the overlord of all our Obas, and that they became independent of him during the Fulani invasion of the Yoruba country. It is equally incorrect to say that Ooni was a mere high priest to the other Obas of our land, especially to the Alaafin of Oyo. There is no history to justify these absolutely erroneous assertions.

His Highness, Ooni Ademiluyi
Commonly known as Ajagun.
Reigned June 1910 - June 1930.
Modakeke broken up on March 27th, 1909, and
was started to be re-peopled by him in 1922

IFE, CRADLE OF THE YORUBA

PART I

Generally speaking, the history of Ile-Ife is, to a certain extent the history of the whole race now called Yoruba race; because from time immemorial, not a single tribe of this vast race has once failed to trace its origin back to Ile-Ife, which they all have acclaimed as the "Eden" of the nation. For this reason, Ile-Ife has earned till this day, among the majority of them, the outstandingly unique honour of being given the enviably peculiar following appellations – (1) Ile-Ife Ile owuro; i.e. Ile-Ife, the land of the most ancient days. (2) Ile-Ife, O-o-daye, *i.e.* Ile-Ife, where the work of creation took place. (3) Ile-Ife, ibiti ojumo ti mo wa, *i.e.* Ile-Ife, where the dawn of the day was first experienced. (4) Ile-Ife, Ori aye gbogbo; *i.e.* Ile-Ife, head of the whole universe.

It was closely round this point that the thought, or belief of the entire people, who are today called Yorubas centred for hundreds of years. On account of this simple belief, not only was Ile-Ife regarded as a sacred place for, and by all of them, but Ooni, its ruler was almost apotheosized, being accorded the position of ranking next to the gods. This was the beginning of the appellation of "Iku-Alase, Ekeji-Orisa", given to the Ooni till this day. Later on, other Obas imitated him in the use of this appellation. This term simply means one who is so high and mighty that, in the power of execution he is next to the gods only.

At that time, immediately after the Coronation Ceremonies of an Ooni he would become the sole property of the Chiefs, to the exclusion of everybody else, including the members of his own family. On all public occasion when Ooni was bound to appear in state, the mere long fence of clothes tied together round him, called 'Paraaso', or at other time, the state umbrella, for that matter, would be seen, when that came into use. Consequently, no Oba had the right of seeing Ooni personally; and they must not even think of visiting Ile-Ife for anything. Therefore, whatever messages that Ooni might have for any Oba, and vice versa, had to be carried to and fro by state messengers.

In those days, not only Ile-Ife and the Ooni were regarded as sacred, but all the Ifes were considered untouchables. Consequently, even though human sacrifices were rife, yet, no Ife man or woman must be offered as a sacrifice to any idol throughout our country. If by a mistake, an Ife man or woman was caught and intended for a sacrifice to a god, he or she would be released immediately it was discovered that he or she was an Ife. This fact could easily be known from the fact that before a person was slaughtered unto a god, he or she had to declare openly before the idol, the tribe and town to which he or she belonged, when offering prayers on behalf of the people who caught him or her, and for the long peace of their town.

Nevertheless, Ifes were sometimes offered in sacrifices to idols if thorough investigations were inadvertently not made before the victims were slain. However, it was the strong exemption which people of other towns took to the Ifes being offered in sacrifices that led to that ancient saying running thus – "Ewo-Orisa, a ki f'omo onile bo ile" i.e. it is forbidden by Orisa that the children of the owner of the land (Oodua) should be offered in sacrifices.

The custom of the Obas of our land not seeing one another personally was a mere imitation of what existed between each one of them and the Ooni in ancient times, until Sir Bernard Bourdillon-Nigeria's fifth Governor, inaugurated the annual Conference of our Obas, and made them to see one another face to face for the first time at the Oyo Conference of 1937.

SLIGHT CHANGES OF THOUGHT

Until the eighties of the last century, not only were we all not known as Yorubas, but it would be a great cause of offence to all Yorubas, whose ancestors came originally from either Mecca or Egypt. Nevertheless, when in the early twenties of the present century, The History of Yorubas by Rev. S. Johnson, the late Pastor of Oyo, came to tell the world that Oodua, the first Ooni of Ife, and the progenitor of all our Obas, with his large following came originally from either Mecca or Egypt to settle at Ile-Ife; several other subsequent writers promptly started to follow the lead of the wrong notion, which ascribed to us all the strange name of Yorubas indiscriminately.

Being spurred by the pride of intelligence of the western education some of those writers as well as their enthusiastic admires, still maintain that there were, at some really unknown periods, when streams of migrations of the Yorubas from somewhere which hitherto, no historian is capable of locating with authority came. Nevertheless, in order to back up their points more stoutly, not only have some writers recently come to tell us that, instead of either Mecca or Egypt, formerly believed as the original home of the Yorubas, there were streams of Yoruba migrations from Sudan; but that in the earliest group of the migrators, some important people like "Luwabi" and "Oluwa", who they believe to have preceded Oodua to Ile-Ife were declared as being kings in their Sudanese original homes before they came to Ile-Ife.

Certainly, if these assertions were true to facts, the oft repeated unreliable stories that have long enshrouded the origin of the word and name 'Yoruba', would have doubtlessly been entirely out of question, because those who have travelled to Sudan to see the original homes of the Yorubas would have before now been fearlessly able to tell us more emphatically about the true origin of the Yorubas than what either Johnson, or any other historians has hitherto been able to do.

Nevertheless, it may be of some interest to know that, from time immemorial, not only was "Oluwa" unknown anywhere in the history of our country, but "Luwabi" was merely used as a common proverbial name in connection with any person, who always act politely, and does his work honestly and meritoriously.

Luwabi was more or less derived from the word or name of "Noah" which is the name of a man, who was remarkably known for his well doing and unflinching fidelity in all things. Consequently, anybody who has acted in the was alluded to above is, from time immemorial termed, "Omoluwabi", that is, a person who has acted as a true son of Noah in imitating him. Therefore, it may not be regarded as an overdone business if it is here stated that the term "Omoluwabi", is yet equally used throughout our extensive country today as it was before. To prove the veracity of this statement, readers are asked to remember how the word "Omoluwabi" is often used in the native song which the late Rev. I.O. Ransome Kuti led the Choir of the Abeokuta Grammar School to render in praise and honour of an old member of the staff of that notable institution, when elevated by the Government, as it is frequently relayed to us in the local radio.

In the face of these facts, as well as in those of the other copious proofs, it cannot be hidden that the name of Luwabi, as an important person did not enter into the history of our race until a few years ago, when a political strongly heated argument arose between the Awujale of Ijebu-Ode and the Akarigbo of Ijebu-Remo. The cause was that, although before this time, both of them used to trace their origin back to Ile-Ife whenever there was any dispute of importance, yet, of recent times, Awujale suddenly said that instead of Oodua, Luwabi was the progenitor of the Ijebus; and that he came originally from Wadai (a place first carved by 300 Arabs) in the Sahara Desert. When coming to settle at Ijebu-Ode, Awujale said, Luwabi passed through Ile-Ife where he gave one of his daughters in marriage to Oodua; and consequently, the Ijebus were related to the Ifes only by affinity; but unlike a few others of the same camp with him, he had not the audacity of saying that Luwabi preceded Oodua to Ile-Ife. But up to date, the opinion of this august person has not enjoyed a hearty general acceptance of all genuine Ijebus who virtually became horror-stricken and highly astonished at the first hearing of the strange story. Notwithstanding Awujale's historical innovation, Akarigbo tenaciously upheld the history of his forefathers by saying openly that his ancestors truly came from no other place than Ile-Ife, and that he knew nothing about Luwabi. This was one of the immediate helpers of the separation of Ijebu-Remo from Ijebu-Ode a few years ago.

The next point that should be carefully noted from the very start of this history is, where the name of "Oodua" was referred as the first Ooni of Ife. In order to clarity this point to some reasonable extent, attention of the readers is drawn to what the Methodist Mission Authorities in Western Nigeria said about the town of Ilesa in 1942, in connection with the celebrations of their work for a hundred years in Nigeria, as contained in a book, entitled "*A Hundred Years In Nigeria*", page 108, and paragraph 1, where they related the story which they heard from the Ijeshas of the time of Haastrup – Ajimoko 1, the Owa of Ilesa (1898-1905), as written below. Title: "*Ilesa The Town*

Of The Iron Sword". A portion of the story – "A young Prince arrived late at a royal feast" so says a Yoruba legend. His father, the powerful Ooni of Ife, was furious at the implied insult. Giving the offender a rusty iron sword, he bade him begun, "Go out into the bush" he roared, "and carve out a kingdom for yourself". With flashing eye and resolute courage, the youth went forth, and created for himself a new town – Ilesa. To this day, the capital of the Ijesha town is known as the town of the "Iron Sword".

Through this story, readers will see that by the expression "the young prince", Orunaja, commonly known as Obokun, the first Owa of Ilesa was meant; and that the words "his father, the powerful Ooni of Ife", Oodua, and no other person was definitely referred to. Consequently, it will be seen why the position of the Ooni as the accredited father of all the other Obas of our land is absolutely indisputable.

Presently, strong hope is cherished that this point will be better dealt with in this history. Nevertheless, it is meanwhile thought much safer to clarify this side of it briefly here so that those who have been misinformed about the true meaning and position of the Ooni among our other Obas from the very inception of our existence as a race, might not be taken aback when these two points come up in future for discussion in their correct values.

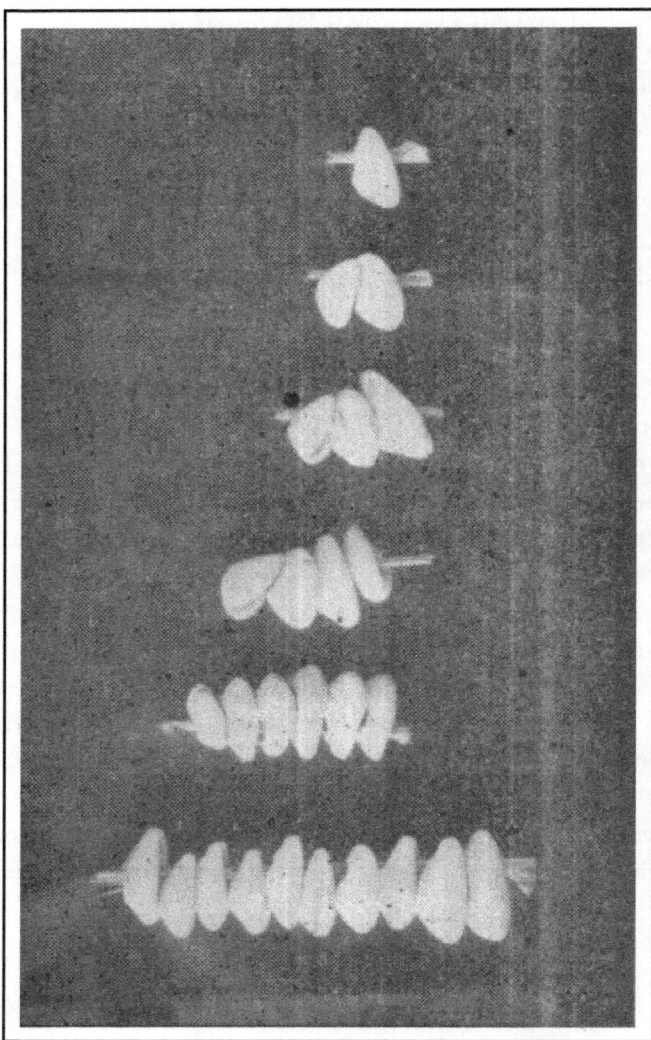

The Ifes' old method and means of sending
messages from one person to another.

ORIGIN OF THE YORUBAS
AS GENERALLY BELIEVED TODAY

Although no historian is hereunto able to say definitely that any of the four places – Mecca, Nubia, Egypt and Sudan, to which the origin of the Yorubas has been traced was the factual original home of the Yorubas, yet, as it has been explained previously, people believe in the migration of Oodua from any of these places to Ile-Ife. To support their arguments, those people frequently allude to the tribal facial marks of our people as being like those of the Egyptians. Similarly, they often refer to some certain carved stones found at Ile-Ife, the manner in which our deads are bound for burial, and the kind of cloth used for them as being entirely identical with those of the Egyptians.

It is definitely sure that these things are likely to be as they are described; but before they are truly accepted as being capable of making us all become Yorubas, whose progenitors migrated from any of the above mentioned places, each of these points will have to be historically gone into and analyzed thoroughly.

As a matter of fact, no one can deny the stubborn fact that Egypt was one of the three important countries of the world, *viz,* Egypt, Mesopotamia, and China, in which civilization was reported to have started. At the same time, nobody can definitely say that there was no civilization in any part of the world at that time, other than in the above mentioned countries; because history clearly tells us that the civilization which grew up on the Island of Aegean Sea, and whose capital was first at Onossus on the Island of Crete, before it was removed to Mycenes, on the mainland of Greece, was in a high standard of efficiency, at least, 1,000 years before the First Dynasty was established in Egypt.

It will perhaps be of some interest to know that, just

as it was in the cases of Egypt and Babylon, so also did the people of these islands find and develop a consummated system of writing; but their writing, which is yet available today is so intricate that no scholar has up to date been able to decipher it.

It is also related that the most enlightened people of the Far East then were the Chinese, who equally established and developed a system of picture writing, hundreds of years ago. It is said that while Western Empires were rising to power, breaking up, and being reconstructed, China had enjoyed 900 years of unbroken progress.

In the face of these facts, it can safely be assumed that in like manner, at the same period, there was a certain amount of civilization in some parts of Nigeria. This outstanding fact was very clear to no less than the august personalities of the type of His Excellency, Sir A.C. Burns, G.C.M.G., one of the retired Governors of the Gold-Coast Colony; Mr. P. Amaury Talbot, one of the high-ranking modern historians, and Professor Leo Frobenius, who have all touchingly referred to the civilization of Ile-Ife as being very very old and realistic one.

Through the profound and keen historical research knowledge of Mr Adewale Thompson, a Lagos Lawyer, not only was he able to corroborate the statements of the above mentioned distinguished and highly accredited historians of recent times, but he also unequivocally said that the foundation of Ile-Ife belonged to the Atlantis period of civilization, which was perhaps the most ancient form of civilization; and therefore, the history of the foundation of Ile-Ife could not be based on any other historic knowledge which was not yet born for thousands of years after Ile-Ife had been in existence.

That the civilization of Ile-Ife was very old and long last is still evidently certain in some parts of the ancient town, where several well set ancient potsherds, used in laying out good roads and properly made courtyards then are yet to be seen in their early, perfect and solid arrangements.

In addition, although the ancient Ifes (now) called Yorubas did not invent and develop the system of any real form of writing yet, like the Chinese, they had a perfect method of sending messages to one another. For example, when cowries had not been introduced into our country by the Portuguese, the Ifes used palm nuts, stringed into fibres in various ways; and when cowries came into use, usage of palm nuts as a means of sending messages was discontinued.

At that time, if a person had a friend or a close relative living in another town, and he wished his friend or relative come back home, he would send six palm nuts or cowries in a string to that friend or relative with a view to telling him that his heart (the addressor) drew earnestly back home that of the addressee.

Six objects used to be sent for this purpose at that time because the word "E-efa", in our language, for which 6, in Arabic, or six in English, stands is from the verb "to draw". Therefore, if the addressee still remained where he was, and the addressor was yet wishing to call him back home, he would send ten palm nuts or ten cowries, as the case might be, in a string to the object of his affection, so as to indicate to him that he earnestly wanted him back home just, in the same way as ten cowries never once failed to achieve their retrieving activities; always commonly expressed in our language thus: "E-ewa ki iwa eni re li awati".

If four cowries were sent to any person, it meant that the addressee should no longer be afraid of what had been agitating his mind, because it had all been turned to a mere laughter. Thus it is seen that the sending of four cowries was a symbol of allaying the fears of the addressee.

The sending of eight cowries to anyone was an indication of the fact that all the members of the family of both addressee and the addressor were quite well and correct in number; and hence, the saying, "Ile jo, Ona jo".

The sending of two cowries in a string in the ordinary way showed that many members of the family of either the sender or the receiver were away from home, or were dead, so much so that it remained the sender of the message alone, or any other person, moving to and fro in too large a space for his size.

If on the other hand, two cowries were sent, "back to back" in a string, it was to show to the receiver that he and the sender were no more on friendly terms, but from that time standing to each other in a back to back manner in all things.

Sometimes, in special cases, red tails of parrots, guinea fowls blue and purple feathered birds, called (Agbe and Aluko's feathers) together with cowries and palm leaves were also used to convey very special messages.

Messages containing red tails of a parrot were sent to the people who had gone to stay in another place for more than their people at home expected them to stay there. Therefore, such messages used to be sent to remind them that though parrots used to fly very extensively in search for food, yet, they never on that account forgot either their tails or their homes without returning to them.

Sending of messages with the feathers of the other two birds simply showed that the senders wished the receivers good luck in their undertakings; because the "Agbe", (blue feathered bird) was reputed for its carrying good things to the god of Ocean, and "Aluko" (purple feathered bird) for carrying good things to the god of Lagoon.

It may be argued that, if Ile-Ife had been in existence, and the age of its civilization was as long as it has been shown before, why are there no remains of mighty ancient buildings found there as are in Egypt and Asia?

In answer to this, readers are reminded that, in very olden times, the knowledge of large imposing buildings was not known in the whole world, until the building of the Tower of Babel; and even that was so flimsy in structure that no trace of it can be found anywhere today.

The actual knowledge of good buildings was not in possession of the people of the world until the Athenians invented, and imparted it to the peoples of Europe and Asia. As the Greeks were once the conqueror of Egypt, it will not be altogether out of place if it is said that Egyptians learn the art of good buildings from them. When, however, on the other hand, it is remembered how until the 15th century, the regarded "Impenetrable" Sahara Desert, had made countries of Africa, south of the Desert to be known by the Europeans as "Dark Continent", inhabited by wild beasts, and evils spirits, and where the sun emitted fire and blood, it will not be difficult to know why, the Ifes of old could not get any civilized country from where to copy the art of good and lasting buildings in ancient times. Thus we see that the chief thing that made the civilization of Egypt, Mesopotamia, and China much more known and universally recognized than that of Ile-Ife was, the privilege of big and navigable rivers enjoyed by those three countries, but of which Ile-Ife was, and up to date still is, destitute. Therefore, so long as Ile-Ife offered attraction to no other people living outside her bounds in this way, there was no incentive for the development of its people's method of sending messages into an actual writing system as those of Egypt and Babylonia.

The Terra-Cotta of the head of Lejua, one of the
ancient Oonis of Ife

ORIGIN OF TRIBAL FACIAL MARKS

Perhaps throughout the whole universe, there is no continent other than Africa, where tribal facial marks have ever been used. This knowledge therefore, reveals that, if the tribal facial mark was an ordination of God, it must have, from the very inception of the world been practiced by all the people of the world.

Historians have it related that, although there are various kinds of tribal facial marks in Nigeria, or in Africa as a whole today, yet, in very ancient times, tribal facial mark of any form was quite unknown in the whole of Africa, which may rightly be considered as one of the momentous sources of slavery.

In order to understand this subject to a certain reasonable extent, it will be necessary to begin its study from some known facts to the unknown ones; or better still from simple to the complex.

Today, in our own country, millions of the children, whose parents have various tribal facial marks have none at all. Yet, there are others, who continue to give their facial marks to their children. If the parents of the first group are asked why they abhor giving their own facial marks to their children as the others still do, the most probable answer they are going to give in return is, "Those facial marks belonged to the days of old when civilization was unknown; but we are now in the days of civilization".

Although the parents who continue to give their facial marks to their children cannot, as promptly as their counterparts, give out the reason for the continuity of their facial marks in their children's faces; yet, they have certain sound and unexpressed reasons for their actions.

The point at issue now is, if indeed, it is the coming of civilization that has made a few millions of people refuse to give the types of their own facial marks to their offsprings, does it mean that, up till now, civilization has not reached the tremendous number of the others, who still give their tribal facial marks to their children?

In the first place, it may be said that those who believe that the stoppage of facial marks in some quarters is largely due to the civilization we now enjoy, are a bit right; because that is one of our acquired things which came to us when we became free to some extent under the British Flag. In the second place, those people may be considered wrong, because the free movement which the world enjoys today does not in any way imply that the world has true civilization. If indeed, there is perfect civilization in the world there will be no war, and there will be no form of oppression. Therefore, in the absence of these pleasing, and everybody liked conditions, it may be rightly said that it is not civilization, but pure abolition of slave trade that has stopped some people from giving their facial marks to their children of modern time.

On the other hand, the people who continue indefinitely marking the faces of their children know, almost as much as the people of the other camp, but the significance which the continuation of the marking of the faces of their children has is, that there is today no such perfect civilization in the world that can prevent waging of war entirely; and for that reason, they have concluded that, wherever warfare continues to exist, slavery is likely, as of old, to put in its nefarious appearance, because they know that originally, slavery was the mother of the various tribal facial marks.

ORIGIN OF SLAVERY

Whenever the case of the origin of slavery comes up for discussions, the thought and belief of many people is, that the Europeans who sold a great many of our people into slavery for over four hundred years were the originators of slave trade in our country. Nevertheless, it should be carefully noted that, although it is hardly feasible to say exactly where, and when slavery first started in the world, yet, we know that its age in Africa is so long that, it may almost be said that Africans were born with it. The fact is, agriculture being one of the most important occupations of the world from its very inception, every man was, right from the beginning, entitled to a piece of land for his farm; but although no one can live for a long time without food, yet, not all men were, and still are willing to labour hard before they eat, or put on clothes; whereas, these things have to be worked for before we get them.

This state of affairs will not at all be regarded as a matter for surprise by anybody, who has known how the earliest men used to get their food by mere drifting from one place to another instead of staying in one place and working hard for it, according to God's command. Nevertheless, in order that such lazy fellows might get something to eat, they craftily began to make themselves servants to the hard working people, who had sufficient to eat and to spare. On the other hand, when those hard working people became men of affluence and honour, they began to be in dire need of people who would help them in their farms as well as in the running of errands therefore, they used more of their food and other things to entice the indolent into their services.

The intensified form of these practices culminated in slavery of the worst kind in the end. Thus we see that the act of those wishing to get those who would be serving them, led some of them to the practice of becoming kidnappers. In later years, kidnapping was so rife among the Africans long before the advent of the Europeans that, they frequently stole away many children belonging to their very close neighbours. As soon as such nearby children were caught, the kidnappers would throw tops, round which were tied some very strong and tenacious strings into their mouths, to prevent noise making. The cord would be tied round their heads with knots on the occiputs.

In order to prevent the parents of such victims from giving cognition to their stolen children again, the kidnappers used to disfigure the faces of those children by giving them any kind of facial marks they fancied. After doing so, they would keep the stolen children in a place, visited by no person than they themselves, until the marks were properly healed up.

In majority of cases, several of such kidnapped children being allowed to come to the view of other people used to know their parents; but the latter; being sure of not having any child with facial marks, used to refuse taking their children if such children happened to escape from their confinements. Nevertheless, there were in later years others, who had been through the experience of others, so careful as to have studied every minute part of the bodies of their children, right from the very inception of the birth of each, that no number of facial marks could entirely prevent them from knowing their children under any circumstances. Therefore, when the stolen children of such careful observers began to escape, and show evident signs of being the children of those careful parents, the latter began to take all possible requisites steps about the matter before they accepted, or rejected any of such children.

When such a practice became a thing of constant occurrence, and more especially, when the inter tribal wars set in their severity of forms, more people commenced to study every part of the bodies of their children more closely in details than ever before.

Finally, when they saw that facial marks were the powerful weapons often mightily utilized by the kidnappers to dispossess them of their children, each tribe started to adopt some special facial marks for its members. Later on, this practice was extended to families of a town, so that the people of a town, or of a family might be easily known and distinguished from those of the others. This method was eventually unanimously adopted in order that less children might be lost than before. Consequently, so long as there was no one wishing to part with his, or her children in the way they had previously been parting with them, each family promptly began to make it a real point of duty to give its members the prescribed facial marks for it. Thus it is seen that, although it is hardly possible to say exactly where or when slavery actually first started in the world, yet, it is known that its age in Africa is so long that it may be said that Africans were almost born with it.

In the Holy Bible, it is stated how the Egyptians enslaved the children of Israel for about 430 long years, and how, before that time, the Egyptians had for many years been dealing in slaves. These points are a clear proof that, the Arabs, who preceded the Portuguese to our land in the wicked trade of human beings, found it with the Africans, and the Europeans were not the starter of the nefarious slave trade in our country.

It should be noted that at first, facial marks were very few in kind, but when those who had not been having facial marks before saw what their other fellows were doing to save their children from being lost entirely, they also joined their more prudent comrades; but in order that there might be less confusion, the latter began to increase the types of the facial marks by applying new kinds to the faces of their children. This is why there are so many different kinds of facial marks in our country today. A few of such kinds are (1) Abaja in sets of three; (2) Abaja in sets of four, and Abaja in sets of six (3) Pele in groups of three; (4) Ture; (5) Abaja in sets of three above and six below;

(6) Variations of the Abaja (7) Keke, or Gombo; (8) Keke or Gombo with the Ibaamu; (9) Abaja Olowu; (10) Keke Olowu; (11) Egba Marks; (12) Ijebu marks; (13) Ijesha marks; (14) Efon marks; (15) Ife marks; (16) Igbomina marks; (17) Yagba marks; (18) Ondo Marks.

Now, so long as we have so many various kinds of facial marks, profusely used in our country, it will be no matter for surprise to anybody if one or two of our facial marks are found to be identical in every respect with that of any other African race. It is however, very gratifying to note that not so many of the facial marks of our land are like those of the Sudanese, because those who recently visited Sudan stated on their return to Nigeria, that the facial marks they saw in Sudan were only exactly like those of the Ogbomosho people, who are only a small fractional part of our whole population.

NECESSITY FOR SLAVES IN EGYPT

In ancient times, Egypt being a common place to which several nations of the world had to go for their supply of food, nearly every inhabitants of Egypt took very seriously to farming. Consequently, the frequent influx of people from various parts of the world made it impossible for the Egyptians alone to cope with the incessant demands of their several customers. In order, therefore, that the Egyptians might be able to slaves from various parts of the world as known to them, to help them in their farm work.

The second thing that made the Egyptians keep several slaves constantly was the daily free labour which everybody was bound to offer the Pharaohs. History reveals that the people of ancient Egypt founded by Mizraim, and whose capital was Memphis, thought their King was a son of the gods, and so called him "Pharaoh", which really means, the place in which he lived. At that time, everything in Egypt belonged to the Pharaohs; and every Egyptian had to work for them, taking such pay as Pharaohs chose to give them.

Wood was as scarce in Egypt as it was among the Sumerians of the valleys of the Tigris and Euphrates; therefore, while the Sumerians were using bricks of mud for their buildings, the Egyptians were using stones for theirs. In order to perpetuate their memories, the kings in those days used to build, during their life times, great tombs called Pyramids because of their shape, in which they were to be laid after death.

Although Menes, who reigned about 3400 B.C. was the first Pharaoh, yet one of the most powerful and most wicked of all Pharaohs was "Khufu", otherwise called "Cheops". Once, Cheops wished to build a very splendid tomb of the type just mentioned above. As the hills of sand covered rocks were above his city, he once saw that the wind had blown the sands from one of those hills, therefore, he thought that that would be a good place for his tomb; for it was high, dry and peaceful. Therefore, he quickly engaged a clever architect, and then sent a vast multitude of slaves – one hundred thousand men to work on the buildings. This great crowd of workers used to work for three months before they returned to their farms and other work. At the end of the third month, another one hundred thousand used to take the place of those who had served their turns.

Although there were no less than seventy Pyramids still to be seen along the Nile today, yet, the one which Cheops built is by far the largest. It stands on a piece of land measuring about seven hundred and fifty feet square. Many of the stone blocks used there weighed between two and three tons each.

The extensive Pyramid of Cheops took thirty years to build. It cost the King very heavy money as well as the lives of numerous slaves; and he did many cruel deeds in order to get enough money and labour. To meet those pressing conditions tactfully, the Egyptians started to get slaves from other countries. That was why slavery became one of the evil necessaries of Egypt in those days.

OUR CONNECTION WITH EGYPT

Hundreds of people, who do not know our real connection with Egypt often propound various theories to support their reasons for believing that we are Yorubas, whose ancestors came originally from Egypt. For the purpose of clarifying this point, it is considered expedient to show to a certain extent here, the following points – (a) the way in which we were connected with Egypt; (b) when and how some of their words entered into ours.

All scholars know that during the abominable slave trade, there were only two ways, *viz*, (1) Desert route, and (2) the Sea route, through which slaves were carried from all countries of Africa to North Africa at the hands of the Arabs, who sold them to the Europeans and Americans.

The European slave trade was started by the Portuguese in a miniature form about A.D. 1441; and although other Europeans who subsequently joined them in the human traffic had long stopped it, yet, the Portuguese continued with it till about 1860, or even a little after that time. During this long span of time, no historian has ever told the world that at a certain period, some Egyptians, or Europeans, or Americans were carried to our country as slaves. Rather, all students of history know that it was only the black people that were carried to the foreign countries mentioned above. If therefore, our ancestors really came from Egypt, some of our people sold there would have known a few, if not many of the relatives of their parents; and more especially so, when the Egyptians saw that the facial marks of many of the slaves were very much exactly like theirs. If the slaves had been so coercely treated that the fear of further tortures did not allow them to ask from the elderly Egyptians as to why their facial marks looked very much like those of the Egyptians, still they would have known this fact through playing or talking with their equals, who would naturally like one way or another, to satisfy their curiosity about the past lives of some of the slaves. On the other hand, Nature is neither so harsh nor unkind as not to have moved somebody in Egypt to probe the lives of the African slaves, as to know why of all people, they were the ones having their exact type of facial marks.

By that, our true connection with Egypt would have been written down in Egypt for the use of the Government, from where many people would have learnt our true connection with either Egypt or Mecca. It would have been very easy to do this, because the first entrance of the Arabs into Egypt in a friendly manner was not earlier than 2,000 B.C. and their actual occupation of the country by the force of arms was in A.D. 641. So long as these dates are definitely known in Egypt, so much so should the exact time of the migrations of the Yorubas from any place, and how the Yorubas adopted the Egyptian facial marks would, have been known.

Nevertheless, it is quite certain, that however difficult the roads might be in those days, not all the carried away slaves died in their lands of bondage; but some of them used actually to return home, except those carried to Europe and America, where Oceans and Seas prevented them from coming back when they made their escapes. Notwithstanding, many of them used to run from one country of Europe to another when they felt uneasy.

If the pitiable plight of the slaves in Egypt, especially during the time of King Cheops, is deeply considered, little shall we wonder that many of our people, who had been slaves in Egypt were forced to make their escapes home whenever possible; and by so doing they brought back with them, some of the Egyptian words which eventually entered into our words through them.

As frequent kidnapping had long taught each tribe or family to adopt special distinguishing tribal facial marks, many of those carried to Egypt had already had their own tribal facial marks on their faces before they were caught and carried away. On the other hand, many of them had not the privilege of coming back home again; and so, when they became wealthy, they paid to their respective owners heavy redemptive money, and they used to give their tribal facial marks in their land of bondage to their children to prove that they were no more slaves, but free born people. This was how, and why some of our facial marks look very much like those of the Egyptians, who were carried away from our land here.

Later on, it will be further proved that more Egyptian words came to us through the Hausas, who used to trade with the people of North Africa, when the road was opened.

MANNER OF BINDING DEADS FOR BURIAL

One of the strong reasons advanced by some writers for believing that our ancestors might have migrated from Egypt to Ile-Ife is, the method of binding our deads for burial, coupled with the kind of cloth used for the burial.

It can in no way be denied by any good student of history that our custom in this respect is, hundred per cent in agreement with that of the Egyptians, for the simple fact that, we are the same black people as the original inhabitants of Egypt; and it is an undeniably stubborn fact that all civilized black people, or black people in general, have certain common characteristics.

Well informed scholars tell us that the chief racial characteristics are – (1) shape of head, (2) texture of hair, (3) colour of eyes and their shape; (4) skin colour, (5) stature; (6) shape of nose and face. Of these the two considered by most people to be of immense importance are the shape of head and the texture of hair. It is also related that there are three main types of hair in the world namely: (a) the wavy hair of the white people; (b) the straight hair of the Chinese; and (c) the woolly or curly hair of the Negroes. Consequently, it is believed, that the three chief races of the world are: (1) a wavy-haired race, with considerable variation in head shape, but usually either markedly broad headed, or long headed. (2) a straight-haired, mostly with broad and round heads; and (3) a woolly-haired race, the majority of whom are long-headed.

It is clearly seen here that the majority of the people of the negro race are long headed and woolly-headed too wherever they may be in the world. Therefore, the markedly prominent long and broad shapes of heads began to appear when there was mixture of white and black races of ancient times through migrations of the black people and the whites into Europe. That of the Atlantis periods of civilization to which some historians believe that the foundation of Ile-Ife belonged, at the time that no history was known in writing anywhere.

To prove to some extent, the time of the mixture of both white and black races through migrations as well as the different kinds of races referred to above, a brief reference will be made to the early history of the United Kingdom of Great Britain and Ireland.

The early history of the United Kingdom of Great Britain and Ireland reveals that, the first set of people to live in Great Britain were called "Paleolithic", or "Ancient Stone" Period people, who used to kill for food, animals of various types with their weapons, made of rough flints, which were several years later found in ancient caves and river-beds in many parts of England, together with the bones of the animals they had killed.

In after years, they were followed by men, who made better weapons, but still of stone. These were called the men of the "Neolithic" *i.e.* "New Stone Period" people. The bones and skeletons of these men were later found buried in long chambers, or borrows (like those of the Egyptians and as well as ours) in many parts of England, Wales, and Ireland, together with polished arrows, hatchets and axes of stones, and needle and pins of bones used by them.

The skull of these men were long and narrow like the skulls of small, dark-skinned, curly-haired people called the "Basques Iberians", who still live in some wild mountainous parts of Spain, and speak a different language from Europe. It is said that there is even a small dark type of men and women among the lowest class kinds of Irish and Welsh of today, which probably is a remnant of these same ancient people.

It is further related that many years after these black people another race with rounder skulls came to mingle with the long-headed people. The skeletons of these people were found in round borrows, formed entirely of earth, and with them were both stone and bronze weapons, showing that they were learning the use of metal. These people were known as "Celtics", and were said to have migrated from Persia, to settle on the British Isles.

Again, scholars tell us that after these people, an Aryan people so called from the old name Aryan (the noble people) anciently applied to part of Persia, started in the East, long before the time of history, spread out into two directions, *viz.*, Persia and India on one side, and across Europe on the other, where we can still follow the traces of their language.

First, these people made their homes a little to the west; then, as they became too numerous, the streams of migration followed on, and parties of them settled farther and farther west till some crossed over the sea into Britain, conquered the inhabitants and settled down as a large-limbed, fair-headed race, among the smaller and darker natives.

Here, history first tells us of them when the Phoenicians, sailing through the Straight of Gibraltar (then called the Pillar of Hercules) about 600 B.C. came to trade for tin with the Scilly Isles, near Cornwall, called by Greek writers, the "Gassiterides", or Tin Islands.

About a hundred years later, the Greeks came overland from Massillies or Marseilles, and at this time, England was called "Albion" and Ireland, "Ierne", while the whole group was called "Britannia". This is how the name "Britain" was gradually arrived at.

Up till now, it is the strong belief of many people that the Romans were the only people who came after the Britons to live in Great Britain and civilized the people; but according to history, the people of that opinion are here to be told that it was about three hundred years after the Greeks had gone before the great Roman General Julius Caesar came to Britain in the years 55 and 54 B.C. In the latter years, he defeated the Britons under their great chief, Cassivelaunus. After making them promise to pay tribute to Rome, he went away again in the last named year.

By this time, the people of the south of Britain had become fairly civilized. They had war-chariots, and fought with spears, spikes and axes defending themselves with a shield of skin and wicker-work. They wore various kinds of clothes, used various types of jewels and lived in scattered huts of wood and reeds on a stone foundation. Each tribe had a din or stronghold, surrounded a wall or high bank for refuge in time of war; and one of these, the "Lynn-din", or lake fort, pronounced "Lundun" – seems to have been the beginning of our today great city of London, capital of England.

It must be chiefly noted that not only were all the people of Britain as well as the Romans pure idol-worshippers at this time, but the Romans had not actually taken occupation of Britain. However, such was the condition of Britain when the Romans came a second time, A.D. 43, under the Emperor Claudius, and took possession of the south of the Island. The Britons struggled bravely for many years, and harassed the Romans in the woods and marshes. For seven clear years, it seemed doubtful which side would win, and then the great British Chief Charactacus, was defeated and sent a prisoner to Rome. When the Romans had once gained a footing, they advanced till in a few years more, they reached the Island of Anglesey, then called Mona, where they massacred the Druids (the idol-priests of the *Britons*) in their stronghold. Notwithstanding, the Romans nearly lost the country; for Boadicea, the widow of a British Chief, roused the people in the east of England, and it was only after London, then an open British town, had been burnt, and the Romans were almost exhausted before they won the day. Queen Boadicea is said to have poisoned herself to escape the shame of being taken.

After this, the Romans ruled over the Britons for about three hundred years. They made good laws, and laid down solid roads, which remain to this day. One of these, called Watling Street, stretched from Dover to Chester, passing through London. They built houses and villages, public baths and theatres: and large towns such as York, Lincoln, and Chester sprang up in different parts of the country. To this day, we can trace many of these towns; e.g.

Doncaster, Manchester by the termination "caster", or "cester" from the Latin word *castra* – a camp or fortified place.

Although no one can tell exactly when Christianity first reached England, yet, it was during this time that missionaries, in the real sense of the word, first visited Great Britain; and both the Romans and the Britons became Christians together.

The Britons lived happily under their conquerirs, imitating Roman customs, speaking Latin as a fashionable language, and relying upon the Romans to defend them. But unfortunately, about 401 A.D., Alaric, King of the Visgoths rigorously attacked Rome. In order, therefore, that the Romans might be able to defend themselves effectively well, they withdrew all their soldiers from Britain, leaving the Britons an easy prey to their other surrounding enemies, who were the "Picts, or Caledonians", and the Scots" who came originally from Ireland, and afterwards gave Scotland its name.

These savage and warlike people had been troubling the Britons and the Romans alike, even when the latter were the masters of the country; therefore, no sooner had the Romans gone than these Picts and Scots broke through the Romans' former defending walls, and harassed the South Britons, who found it difficult to defend themselves. There and then, they sent for the Roman soldiers to defend them; but in the year 410 A.D., the Romans withdrew entirely, and left the Britons finally to their fate.

This brings us to the point where the history of England begins, for the Britons, in their despair, invited some more powerful enemies, who were hovering about their shores to come and help them. These terrible enemies were the English ancestors, who founded the English Nations, and we must learn now where they came from, and how they came.

As it was previously stated, for more than a hundred years before the Romans left Britain, they had been much troubled by the pirates, who came in large flat – bottomed boats across the German Ocean from the country around the River Elbe. So fierce and cruel were these Saxon pirates that the Romans built strong fortresses from the River Humber all round to Vectis or the Isles of White, to keep them away.

The invaders belonged to the Teutonic race, quite different from the Celts, although they came originally from the same stock in the East. As the Celts drove out a part of those whom they met in Britain, so also they drove the Celts whom they met on the plains of Germany as far as the Romans would let them, and then made their way north-wards to the country between the rivers Weser and Elbe, and up into Jutland, Sweden and Norway.

The Britons fought against these unyielding enemies for at least forty years after the departure of the Romans. At last, however, worn out by the attacks of the Picts and Scots by land, and those of the Saxon pirates by sea, the Britons resolved to set one enemy against the other; and a British Chief named Votigern is reported to have invited in the year 449 A.D. Hengist and Horsa, two Chiefs of the sea pirates from Jutland, to settle in the Isles of Thamet, in the north of Kent, and fight his battles against the Picts. The Jutes did as they were asked to, but no sooner had they overcome the Picts than they turned their arms against the Britons themselves. Horsa was killed in the first battle, but Hengist led the Jutes on, and after thirty years of heavy fighting, his son Eric, founded the two small kingdoms of East and West Kent, of which the chief city was Cantwarebyrig, or Kentmensborough, now the city of Canterbury.

By this act, the Jutes were the first ancestors of the English people to settle in Britain. Next to them were the

Saxons, who came in the year 477 A.D. from the opposite shores between the Rivers Elbe and Weser, to land with their Chiefs Elle and Cissa on the south-coast of Britain near the Roman city of Regmum. This city received from Cissa the name of Cissanncester, afterwards, Chichester.

Long before this, the Britons had bitterly regretted calling for the assistance of foreign allies, for these invaders killed, or drove back, all who were before them, and when Cissa took the town of Anderida, near where Pevensey now is, he left not a single living Briton. In occupying the country, the Saxons moved forward very slowly, for the land was covered with dense forests, marshes and swamps. The Britons fought desperately against them before they were eventually overcome.

Although it took the Saxons sixty long years to win Southern Britain, yet, at the end of that time, they had founded the kingdoms of the South Saxons or Sussex, West Saxons or Essex, and Middle Saxons or Middlex, and the Britons were driven westwards into the parts now called Somerset, Devon, and Cornwall. Meanwhile, on the north-east of Britain, another tribe, called the "Angels", who came from the small country of Angeln in Schleswing, north of the River Eyder, were settling down in large numbers. This tribe is noteworthy for two things which are, (1) almost the entire people came over with all they had, and made Britain their home, and (2) they gave their name of Angles to the country now called England.

We do not know really when they first landed, but it is known that some of them sailed up the Humber, and founded a kingdom called Deira; while in 547 A.D. another portion of this tribe came in fifty boats from Angeln, under a chief called "Ida, the flame-bearer" and going farther north, founded the kingdom of Bernicia; and after a struggle of fifty or more years, Bernicia and Beira were united in

603 A.D. into the kingdom of North-Humber-land, which cited from the River Humber, right up to the Firth of Forth.

This explains why the Lowland Scotch are Teutons, while the Highlanders are Cells. The Angles drove the Celts into the Highlands and too kthe Lowlands for themselves, and the city of Edingburgh itself took "Eadwinesburh", from one of the later Anglian kings, named "Eadwube, or Edwin".

Meanwhile, other Angles were settling to the south of the Humber. The North-Folk and South-Folk settled in the countries still called by their name, and formed the kingdom of East Angelia; while others pushed into the middle of England, into that part now called the Midlands Counties. These Middle-Angles were called March-men or Bordermen, while their land was called March-land, or Mercia. Thus it is known that about two hundred years after the Romans had left Britain, the Britons had been driven right over to the west of England, Devonshire and Cornwall on the South, into the mountains of north Wales on the west, and into Cumberland, Westmoreland, and Lancashire, then called "Strathcyde". They also began about this time to be called "Welsh" *(used for them by the Angles as if they were strangers, or those whose language they did not understand)*. The rest of the country was in the hands of the Jutes, Angles and Saxons, who were all called Saxons by others, but among themselves, more commonly as "English".

The southern country from the English Channel to the Firth of Forth was firmly held by them, and it was roughly divided into seven chief kingdoms like Kent, belonging to the Jutes; Sussex, Wessex and Essex, belonging to the Saxons; Northumbria, Angelia, and Mercia, belonging to the Angles, and these seven kingdom were given the common name of "Heptarchy". Meaning a government by seven men.

REASONS FOR REFERENCE TO ENGLISH HISTORY

It may be a great matter for surprise to many readers that when studying the history of our race, the history of England has been so profusely referred to. It is a well-known fact to all students of history that England has had a very immense share in the making and shaping of Africa in general, and of Nigeria in particular. As such, it is thought necessary to link the history of our country with that of England to a certain extent; because although the Portuguese, and not the English sailors, had the credit of the discovery of Tropical Africa, yet, English sailors, after the sixteen century, gradually took the front place among the other European nations that had dealings with Africans.

It is an undeniably stubborn fact that the English had the largest share in the nefarious slave trade before its abolition; but equally so is it their prodigious credit for being the nation which did the most to abolish it. On the other hand, the English history is chiefly brought into play here because, it is a reasonable opinion that before a judge can judiciously decide a case, he must needs hear clearly the two sides of it. Therefore, before credence can truly be accorded the recently so much talked of, streams of Yoruba migration from somewhere to Ile-Ife, it is thought necessary that the attention of the reading public be drawn to some other places where streams of such migrations really took place thousands of years ago, so as to know the true nature of various types of migration. To do these things creditably well, it is believed that no other thing than thorough references to the history of England can satisfy the most urgently needed points of truth.

As contained in the part of the English history already referred to, not only the various types of peoples who had lived in England for thousands of years before the ancestors of the English, whose name the country now bears were, and still are known, but it is also clearly depicted that owing to the incapability of the Britons to cope with their two powerful enemies on the land on the one hand, and on the sea on the other, they sent to the two leaders of the Jutes-Hengist and Horsa, from Jutland for help against the Picts and Scots. It is clearly pointed out how the invitees eventually turned their destructive swords against their invitors; and for how long they both struggled hard before the Jutes gained ascendancy, is an open secret. The first two towns built by Eric, son of Hengist, are still known today. It has been clearly shown how the Saxons and Angles subsequently came to settle in England, and how long it took them to settle properly. Equally so have the names of the different leaders of the groups of the peoples who came before the English and the Romans been shown, together with the original languages spoken by each of the groups, and where the remainder of those could still be found today, using their indigenous languages, notwithstanding the universality of the usage of the English language for them all. Along with these, the important work done by each group of the migration is clearly revealed. Mention is also definitely made of the Roman, Jute, Saxon and the Angle leaders, who came to occupy the country, and the notable towns and streets built by some of them as well as the names given to them, with reasons for them are shown.

Perhaps the most noticeable of all these points were (1) the perpetual retainment of their original languages, and (2) their long practice of non-fraternization with one another. It was an open secret that it was in no way possible for any of the migrators to England to forget his original language consequently; their original languages were, and still are, so valuable and dear to them that they are even proudly still spoken today by the remnants of them wherever they are. Thus we see that apart from English, which is the common language of the whole people of the United Kingdom, the Irish and the Highlanders in the north of England, still speak "Gaelic", and the Welsh speak "Cymric" freely among themselves today, where other people will be mere on-lookers. Apart from these, it is to be remarked that the remnant of the dark-skinned people, who migrated to Europe, thousands of years ago, are yet to be seen with their wooly or curly hair, upon which no climatic condition ahs even had any effect.

It is highly of immense importance to note that though some of them, like the Jutes, Saxons and the Angles, were originally of the same stock, just as the Irish and the Highlanders were of the same stock, yet, it was not at first possible for them to live together as amicably as the Ifes (now called) Yorubas started to live peacefully and harmoniously under the sole Kingship of Oodua, so much so that, until this day, they all acclaim him as their father and not as an ordinary leader.

It must again be taken notice of that, until a little over 800 years ago, it was not at all in the calculation of the Welsh to be in the same camp with the English in any sphere of work. It was after the English completely conquered them, that they partially submitted to their conquerors. It was the democratic form of government that eventually helped to bring them much closer to one another as they are today. In like manner, the English and the Scottish had nothing in common until 1608, when the reign of King James 1 of England, whose father was a Scotch King, and whose mother, Queen Mary of Scots, was an English Princess, united the two Kingdoms together, because James was the King of the two countries after the death of Queen Elizabeth I, in 1603.

It will be recalled that, before the earliest seven English kingdoms could be reduced to one solid kingdom, there were series of warfares, in which one king killed the other in almost regular successions, until it remained only one ruler over the whole country as it is today; but historically, in our country, contrary was the case from the very beginning of our existence.

As a matter of fact, it cannot be expected that migrations would be entirely of the same type in every way; nevertheless, many and varied as they might be, they all must have a few things in common. Therefore, one of the reasons why the likely possible streams of the migration of the Yorubas from a yet unknown origin to Ile-Ife is regarded as purely incredible one by some historians is, the way in which many of the peculiar characteristics of a true migration are altogether out of the history of the migrations of the Yorubas, who were supposed to have come in several sections, under different leaders, who are thought to have come to settle only at Ile-Ife as a body of people under only one King – Oodua. Therefore, it is considered by some writers that the migration of the Ifes (now called Yorubas) from Egypt, or Mecca, or Nubia, or Sudan to Ile-Ife will be nothing short of a mere farce until its believers are able to declare categorically the following points –

(1) the actual original homestead of the Yorubas; (2) the other countries of the world by which the original Yoruba country was bounded on its four corners; (3) the true origin of the word and the name Yoruba with meanings; (4) whether the migrators were known by the name "Yoruba" or by any other name in their original home, or they came to acquire it out here; (5) if they were known as Yorubas before they came here, where in the world can their remnant be found today? (6) If they had a different other name or language before they came here, what was the name or language? (7) If they acquired the name Yoruba out here, what occasioned it? (8) When they came before Oodua, whom they did not know before, how was

it possible and easy for them all to be peaceful under his sole rule for so many years without much hitch before and after they had gone to their present localities at his main and absolute command? (9) The names of the various types of people, whom the Yorubas came to meet at Ile-Ife should be given. (10) The names and places of the wars which the Yorubas waged with the people before they gained ascendancy should equally be known. (11) It should be clearly stated whether the people surrendered of their own accord, or whether under the pressure of the Yorubas. (12) We should know where the remnant of those people are today if they were not entirely massacred, and if they were, the battle at which they were so destroyed, and the leaders of both sides should be known.

It may perhaps strongly be argued that lack of knowledge of writing among them in those days could not have allowed the knowledge of such facts to be in possession of anybody today. To disprove this point, it will be remembered that though the minutest part of the English history is well-known today, yet knowledge of writing was entirely unknown in Great Britain until many years after the Roman occupation of the country. Still, truth does not allow us to accept to plea of ignorance of writing among the early Yorubas so to speak, from the fact that, notwithstanding the lack of knowledge of writing among the ancient Ifes, the story of the Igbos, who used to come periodically to kidnap the Ifes is well-known everywhere in our country till today. Nevertheless, that the Igbos themselves were real Ifes, will later be proved in this history.

Oronmiyan,
the most popular staff of the Ooni of Ife

CARVED STONES AT ILE-IFE

Failure to know exactly the true origin of the Yorubas, and who made the surprisingly carved stones and Terra Cottas of Ile-Ife, and being unable to know the purpose for which they were marvelously carved and made, caused many people to think Egypt was the place from which the Yorubas must have migrated to Ile-Ife. The same reason led many writers to the narrow idea of saying that those wonderful carvings were not done by the ancient Ifes, and that if, indeed they were carved by the ancient Ifes, why can't the Ifes of today do the same?

In answering the people of such a school of thought, their attention is called to the following points: (1) It is a well-known fact that very many rich people sometimes have their money entirely and thoughtlessly spent off, and their whole property altogether spoiled and wasted by their children, soon after their death. Can it therefore, be rightly said by anybody that the parents of such children were in their lifetimes not very rich? (2) In the second place, many a brilliant and erudite scholar has been known to have very dull and lazy children. Can it on account of that be correctly said that so long as those children are dull and lazy, it shows that their father was not in his life-time a very good scholar?

Before going further in this line, readers are requested to note that the knowledge of carving either wood or stones is not a new thing to the Ifes at all. The fact that the Ifes of today are not as important in the work of art, or carving, or of war, and in numerical strength as their great grandfathers were, does not mean that they were not once the head and leaders of the whole of the people known as Yorubas today, because history definitely tells us that during the time that the Ifes founded the town of Ibadan the third time, they were the most numerous of all, having the best and most powerful soldiers in the whole country. They were the leaders with whom the Ijebus and the Oyos stayed then. Therefore, the fact that the Ifes of today do not take to such carving works as were done by the ancient Ifes does not in any way suggest that the so much talked of carved stones of Ile-Ife were not carved by the ancient Ifes, but by some unknown foreign people.

DIDI-OTA (ART OF HUMAN BEINGS BECOMING STONE)

Throughout the whole of our extensive country, there was not a town in ancient time in which the idea of Ota-dida was not well-known. Although it has long been abandoned, yet, the true meaning of the term is still quite understood by a few people today. Therefore, before it is briefly explained why the Ifes of today to not take to stone-carving and Terra-Cotta – making, it will be necessary to know something about this art of becoming stones.

The story of Obalufon-Ogbodirin as will be seen elsewhere in this history, will partially show to the readers that many ancient Ifes were privileged to live to very great ages, and by this privilege, they made many people believed that they never died at all. Obalufon-Ogbodirin himself was one of the typical examples. In order therefore, that they might be able to bring their tendentious purposes into actual operation, they used to make some carved stones in their own effigies, and keep them in some secret places which would be known to only a few trusted people under them. Any important aged person who had done this would tell his most trusted few people where he would like his corpse be secretly buried, and where his cenotaph would be placed to show to the world how powerful he was. This practice is termed "Did'ota". "The verb of these words is "da" i.e. to become: and the *noun* of it is, "Ota", from

"Okuta", stone and hence, "D'ota" means – "become stone".

At that time, people who could so deceive others in this way were highly esteemed as men of great honour and respect. The honour and respect so accorded them frequently induced many other people to follow their ways of life. This was why the term "Did'ota" was widely known throughout our country in those days. Eventually, when people wanted to speak of the long age of any of the people who had so cleverly deceived others into the idea of being magically turned into stone, they used to express it Hyperbolically thus: "O gbogbo, O di ota" i.e. he was so old that he eventually became a stone.

When many people from outside the town of Ile-Ife began to hear of the fame of many Ifes in this way, they also coveted and copied them, just almost as some wild tribes from north-west suddenly went upon, and conquered the Sumerians, whose arts of writing, building, and preserving things, they quickly adopted.

Fortunately for the Ifes, the people who adopted their ways of doing things having regarded Ile-Ife as their original home, did not attempt capturing it then, but went there to learn various arts. For instance, the art of brass casting was never known in Benin City until the reign of Oba Oguola. As a proof of this, *vide A Short History Of Benin*, page 18 paragraph. 3, where it reads thus: "Oba Oguola wished to introduce brass casting into Benin, similar to various works of art sent him from Uhe (Ile-Ife). He therefore, sent to the Oghene of Uhe, (Ooni of Ife) for a brass – smith, and Igue-igha was sent to him. Igue-igha was very clever and left many designs to his successors, and was in consequence defiled, and is worshipped till this day by the brass smiths. The practice of making brass castings for the preservation of the records of event was originated during the reign of Oguola".

Thousands of people believe that the various works of art done in Benin were introduced there by the Portuguese. This is in no way true to fact. Those artiste works were only encouraged by the Oba of Benin when John Alffonso d'Aveiro opened a foreign trade with the Binis in 1485-6 A.D. As a proof of this, vide the same history book of Benin, page 39, paragraph 2, where it reads thus: "Esigie encouraged and improved the brass work which had been introduced to Benin by Oba Oguola". Page 33, and paragraph 4, of the same history book reads thus: "A Portuguese, named John Alffonso d'Aveiro, visited Benin City for the first time in 1485-6, during this reign; he introduced guns and cocoanuts into this country".

These references show clearly (1) that the various work of art of Benin were taught to the Binis by the ancient Ifes, and not by the Portuguese, who met them there. (2) That not only did the Ife carvers become rich, but had many apprentices from outside the town of Ile-Ife. The in-rush of the outside people made more people to pay better attention to the art of carving in almost every part of our country. This is why some carved stones are also found in some towns other than Ile-Ife today.

Though the reasons of not finding a single Ife, who can boast of the knowledge of such carving work today as those carried on by the ancient Ifes are many, yet, mention will be made of only a few of them here as follows:

(1) Those carvings were originally made as cenotaphs to represent the men and women who tried to make people believe that they were not actually dead, but were magically transformed into stones. But in the process of time, their secrets being known to many other people, the carvers had very few people to patronize them as before. Gradually, they lost the patronage of their entire customers.

(2) The work of carving is not an ordinary one. It requires heavy expenditure of time, much thinking, and

enormous physical activities. Therefore, there being no more markets again for such carvings anywhere in those days, the carvers began to relax their interest in the work, and in course of time, it was partially forgotten.

Next to that, the Ifes first took to wood and ivory carving to represent some idols as they used carved stones to represent human beings; because wood and ivory were much easier to carve than stone, on which their ancestors had been working. But again money being not forthcoming as they expected, and ivory being not easy to get, many wood and ivory carvers gave up their profession. As a matter fact, these were not done all at once; because carving was still left in the hands of a few people, chief among those who were the members of a family known and called, "Agbeke" meaning, ivory carvers, or dressers of ivory, into artistic designs and, consequently. "Ike", means the finished work of an ivory dresser.

It will perhaps interest the readers to know that not only the art of carving stone, wood, and ivory was known by the ancient Ifes, but some of them were keenly interested in the art iron casting too. The place where their irons were melted is till this day called "Ileru" (Furnace). It is today at a place very close to the site of the first Anglican Church, built at a part of Ile-Ife, called Iyekere by the Ifes and the Modakekes through the order of the late Bishop C. Phillips of Ondo, who stationed Mr (afterwards) Rev E.A. Kayode, the paternal grand-father of Mr Fani-Kayode there as the first clergyman of Ife in 1899. The new road, constructed from the old Ogunsua Market in Modakeke to join Iraye or Amola Road passes through the remaining hill of the lava produced from that furnace when it was in full operation.

It must again be noted that as the art of stone, wood and ivory carving was in course of time forgotten, so also was the art of iron melting eventually forgotten and lost, just as the ancient Cretian writing, whose meaning still remains unintelligible to scholars is regarded as being lost today. Nevertheless, there is a tremendous lesson here for the whole Ifes everywhere to learn. Everyone should begin to think things out in modern lines as his ancestors did in times of old. When Ifes are referred to, it must be understood that the whole people now called Yorubas are meant. It does not in the least mean that they all cannot think deep enough to bring profitable things out, but the trouble with us is, that the plenty of fanciful things we daily see around us have so made us satisfied that , most of us have become those who always wait for things to happen, instead of those who should make things to happen as their ancestors had been.

It is said that practice makes perfect; but it all depends on how one practices. If we practice aright with fortitude, w e shall surely eventually be perfect; or has it not been well said by Samuel Smile thus – "National progress is the sum of individual industry, energy, and uprightness, as national decay is of individual idleness, selfishness, and vice?"

RECENT VIEWS OF SOME WRITERS

Apart from all that has been said above, it was not long ago observed that on account of a book published just a few years ago, many people still believe that we came from Egypt or Mecca. Those who still believe that we are Yorubas, who came originally from Egypt gave, among other reasons that, as every Yoruba man uses some words always as his own language, we must always trace our origin to Egypt. Some of the words they so referred to are, Amin, Alafia, Wahala, Fitila, Amo, Aroye, Gafara, Barika, Lakai, Gasikia, To-o, Jamba, Manafiki, Dukia.

They maintain that we should always trace our origin

to Egypt through the Hausas, because these words are more or less Egyptian words, which our ancestors brought with them when coming to Ile-Ife. It must nevertheless be realised that although the above quoted words are freely used in our daily speeches today yet, they are incapable of making us to trace our origin to Egypt, because as it has been pointed out already, those words entered into our language through trade intercourse, and through some of our people who managed one way or another to escape from their lands of bondage, and came back to stay with their people. On the other hand, it does not mean that if there was no trade dealing with the Hausas, we could not have got equivalent words to use among ourselves for the above-referred to words. Their equivalents in our words are – (1) In our language, "Amin" means "Ase, or K'ose be-e". (2) "Lafia", which is turned to Alafia, means "Se daadaa ni gbogbo ile ati nkan wa?" (3) "Amo", means, "Sugbon". (4) "Gafara", means, "Mo bere af'rijio o." (5) "Barika", means, "Ma-a rora, or Ma-a wole". (6) "Lakai", means, "Ogbon tabi imoye", (7) "Aroye", means, "Ebe, tabi oro ti a tenumo iso lera-lera". (8)"Gasikiya" means, "Otito ponyanun". (9) "To-o" means, "Ko buru, tabi o dara be-e". (10) "Jamba", means, "Iwa ibi, tabi iwa buburu si omo-enikeji eni". (11) "Wahala", means, "Aibale okan, tabi iyonu". (12) "Fitila", means, "Atupa". (13) "Manafiki", means, "Arekereke" tabi "Tembelekun". (14) "Dukia", means, "Ohun ini". (15) "Koowa", means, "Olukuluku". (16) "Barika", means, "O ku ewu, tabi o ku orire".

Although through our long dealings with the British people, some English words like 3*d*, which we call "Toro", 6*d*, which we call "Sisi", 9*d*, to which we give the name of "Nain" and, 1*s* which we often call "Sile kan", have entered our language, yet they are incapable of making us become true English people. Therefore, it is considered that, if the believers in the migration of the Yorubas from Egypt still maintain that the previously quoted words are capable of making us real Yorubas, whose ancestors came from Egypt, because we often use those words, then, the English people will likewise be forced to trace their origin to nearly all the countries of the world from where they have borrowed the following under-mentioned words:

(1) From America they borrowed – Alpaca, cannibal, lema, and tobacco.

(2) From China – Gong, nanki, tea, typhoon.

(3) From Hebrew – Cherub, cinnamon, jubilee, sabbath, seraph, shekel.

(4) From German – Plunder, quartz, swindler, waltz, zinc.

(5) From Arabia – Admiral, algebra, chemistry, harem, sofa, zero.

(6) From Hindoo – Benian, Betel, calico, muslin, raja, rupee.

(7) From Persia – Sugar, Bazaar, caravan, jackal, jasmine, pasha, shawl.

(8) From Italy – Bandit, cameo, cartoon, gondola, portico, umbrella.

(9) From Malay – Bamboo, mango, orang-out-ango, sago.

(10) From Portuguese – Caste, fetish, mandarin, pagoda, verandah, yarn.

(11) From Spanish – Alligator, cargo, cigar, cork, grandee, mosquito, potato.

(12) From Turkish – Bey, cadi, horde, khan, seraglio, tulip, turban.

Knowing full well that the fore-going points are insufficient to make us Yorubas as many people think it to be, some more seriously thinking people began to ask lecturers and writers of Yoruba history, to tell the world definitely the following things – (a) whether or not, we were originally Yorubas, whose ancestors came from either

Egypt or Mecca, (b) how we came about the name Yoruba, and what the real meaning of the word Yoruba is.

It was very easy for many people to answer the first question promptly, because The History of the Yorubas, page 5, and a portion of paragraph 1, reads thus – "The Yorubas are certainly not of the Arabian family, and could not have come from Mecca, that is to say the Mecca universally known in history, and no such accounts as the above are to be found in the records of Arabian writers of any kings of Mecca; an event of such importance could hardly have passed unnoticed by their historians."

In order that he might be able to put a final stop to such agitating questions once for all, one of the accredited modern writers of Yoruba History – Chief Samuel Ojo, the Bada of Shaki, on page 21, of his book, entitled, "The Origin of the Yorubas" answered the second question by giving two reasons why we are called Yorubas today in the following statements–

(a) "Two derivations are given to us about the name "Yoruba"; they both lead to Prince Oranmiyan. Ife story says, when Oranmiyan was born, on the right hand, from head to foot, was brown on the left, from head to foot was black. Father Oodua said, "Ode de, Oranmiyan, niti Yoruba" (Hunter comes, my grievance is over about Yarrooba, the one who would avenge from Yoruba comes). Since then, Oranmiyan has been called Yarroobah, contracted to Yoruba".

(b) "The second story says: When Yorubas first came to Ile-Ife, they were not called Yorubas, neither Ifes, but when Oranmiyan, waged war against the powerful Yoruba in Egypt, and conquered him, it was a great astonishment to the South and North of Nigeria, so that the question ran as this – "Oranmiyan segun Yorroobah?" Since then they began to call Oranmiyan Asegun Yarroobah (Conqueror of Yarroobah), gradually, Oranmiyan and

Asegun were cut off, and Yoruba, as the above, retained up to date".

Definitely, this is another point which shows that, originally, we were not Yorubas whose ancestors came under the leadership of Oodua to settle at Ile-Ife because (1) up to this day, Oodua, and not Oranmiyan is still believed to be the father of all our Obas and race. (2) He is believed by all historians, except Chief Ojo, as the one who migrated from somewhere to Ile-Ife. (3) Oranmiyan on the other hand, was born and bred as the youngest and last son of Oodua at Ile-Ife where he reigned as the Ooni of Ife.

Therefore, if the name Yoruba came to us all through him, what was the name by which our ancestors were known before he was born, and when he was young, so long as they were not known as Ifes or Yorubas? (4) If on account of Oranmiyan's victory over a man called Yarroobah in Egypt, he consequently acquired the name Yoruba, it would have remained his sole personal appellation, and should not have become our racial name, because we all did not come from him as we came from Oodua.

If there was a man called Yarroobah, whom Oranmiyan conquered in Egypt, not only should his real town or country have been known and written down by the Government, according to the ancient standing rule of Egypt; but the people who first came to Ile-Ife from Egypt should have been known as Yorubas, and not as Ifes, who did not come from Egypt, fight from the beginning. Consequently, not only Yorubas, but Yorubas proper should have started from Ile-Ife, and with the Ifes, instead of from Oyo, and with the Oyos, who claimed Oranmiyan as their progenitor, on account of the temporary protection which he offered the Oyo people when he was sent by Ooni Obalufon-Ogbodirin to help Oloyo out of his then grave situation. However, later in this history, it will be proved how, originally, the word Yoruba was the name of no race until it was in a curious way applied to the Oyos for a certain purpose. It will be further proved that Yoruba was applied to us all by the early Missionaries of the Anglican Denomination. In like manner, it will be revealed how and when Oranmiyan became the adopted progenitor of the Oyos.

The Name of Yoruba

Memory is apt to be short. Many people are likely to grow careless about several things which their fathers and grandfathers had known so well as they knew their own fingers. Nevertheless, facts, being facts, they must one day come out one way or another and must consequently be told, however bitter or strange they may perhaps sound to many people.

When Africans were in those horrible days of slave trade being carried away by thousands to Europe, America, and West Indies, as well as North Africa, as hopeless creatures, their purchasers and subsequent owners had no other better name for them than the one which their dark skins suggested; and hence, we black people were first known to the rest people of the world by the common name of "Negroes", which undoubtedly means, "Black People", from Latin word "Nigger".

When through the very powerful instrumentality of the selfless and philanthropic work of Clackson, William Wilberforce, Thomas Fowell Boxton, of the blessed memory, the British Government was moved to pass an effective law, forbidding further prosecution of the nefarious slave trade in the whole of the British Empire, not only did they make Sierra-Leone a separate settlement for the slaves freed, but they also made it their incumbent duty to rescue as many slaves as they could, from the hands of the other European and American nations, who would then not like to give up that wicked trade. As a result of this generous and cordial move, the British Government was able to capture 1,077 slave-ships of the other nations between the years 1829 and 1849, and set free all their cargoes. All the slaves thus rescued and set free were later given the name of "Sierra Leonians".

The name Sierra Leone *(from which their name was derived),* was first given to that Colony by the Portuguese explorers. This was principally so, owing to the strong resemblance in shape which one of the mountains there bears to the King of beasts; and hence, Sierra Leone, means, **Lion Mountain.** But in order perhaps, to mark the circumstances leading the British Government to this place, they gave the name Freetown to the capital of the whole place.

Besides that, all the freed slaves drawn from any of the towns forming our today Yoruba country, were given the distinctive name of "Aku", or "Oku", either of which was derived from their peculiar way of saluting one another thus – "O or E", for singular, and when pluralized, "A or E" contracted from "Oku-ewu" and "E ku-ewu" respectively.

Our ancestors regarded every stage of the life of an individual as being surrounded by perils every moment; therefore, everyone who happened to see any period of the day, that is, morning, afternoon, and evening, and even from moment to moment, was always considered lucky; and hence, the greetings of "O ku-ewu", or "A ku-ewu owuro, osan" and "ale", respectively.

These greetings are not often clearly expressed in meaning when used; but their import and correct usage are vividly revealed in the Expression "E ku-ewu odun; e ku-alaja odun"; where the word "alaja" means, going through the period of a year.

In meaning, these expressions really imply, "I congratulate you for the fortune which has enabled you to see this particular period, after passing through the previous surroundings dangers." This idea led us all to our frequent greetings of "E ku-owuro, e ku-osan", and "e ku-ale", respectively.

Realizing the full meaning of these salutations, our people in Sierra Leone used to include themselves in the congratulations offered to others, almost more than the people out here used them, because they wished well for themselves too. That was why they used to say "A ku", when saluting one another.

Before that time, the Europeans and the Americans had no other name for the whole people of Africa than "Africans," but as our people in Sierra Leone were particularly known for their frequent use of the word "A ku" in saluting one another, they were given the nickname of "A ku" in order to distinguish them from the other African groups. Eventually, not only that the Europeans chose to give them "A ku" as their permanent and racial name, but they themselves gladly took it as such. That is why they continued using it as such till 1843 that Mr S.A. *(afterwards)* Bishop Ajayi-Crowther introduced "Yoruba" to them as their racial name.

When some of our people were fortunate to return to Lagos and districts from Brazil, they carried back with them, the name of "Inagoes", which is a corrupt form of the word "Negro", by which they were known and called in their land of bondage. From that time, not only they, but the rest people of Lagos came to be known as "Inagoes" through the influence of the immigrants who were more civilized than those whom they came to meet. Consequently, all the vernacular books written and used in Lagos then were called "Iwe-Inago" (Inago Books) by the natives, though in following Crowther's idea, the missionaries insisted on calling them Yoruba Books. In like manner, when the liberated Egbas first came back to Abeokuta from Sierra Leone in 1839, they gave the name of "Iwe Egba" (Egba Books) to all the books written afterwards in Abeokuta in their language, and their language itself was then known and called "Ede-Egba", as from 1847, when the Anglican Missionaries became properly settled there.

Those freed slaves were able to do these things for the following reasons – (1) As a result of the long and devastating internecine wars, the idea of regarding themselves as separate entities was more prominent in their minds than they thought of a united strong body of people for a common suitable name for us all. (2) The intention of both the early missionaries and Governor, Sir Alfred C. Moloney who jointly fathered the idea of calling us all Yorubas wishing to give them a common name of Yoruba, were not clear to them; and above all, the people to whom they wanted to give the name were not at all informed of it before they applied it. (3) Were they then as settled as they now are, they would have had no hesitation in giving "Ife" as their original appropriate common name, should they have been consulted before "Yoruba" , was indiscriminately given them. (4) The word "Yoruba" was nothing short of pure Greek to no less than 99% of the people now called Yorubas, when they first heard it being used for them as a common name because up to that time, the name "Yoruba" was known and used by only a few people in the Oyo division.

It will perhaps be of some interest to a few readers if they are told that, as a result of this, many aged people of Abeokuta, Ijebu, Ile-Ife, Ilesa, Ekiti and Ondo had, and still have a very strong aversion for being known and called "Yoruba". The truth of this can still be tested even among the uneducated Ibadans as well as those of other towns of our country. This class of people very strongly hates to hear that even the Ifes are ranked with the Yorubas; how much more then of the other tribes.

INAGO PEOPLE

Some people who do not know that the people who are today called "Inagoes" in the French Territory were formerly part of our people, who came back from Brazil to settle with their people in Lagos now consider them to be a separate tribe from us, as if they were not part of those who came from Ile-Ife. For the clarification of this point, it is thought necessary to say that, when some of them, like those of Lagos, first came, they dealt so freely with the people of Lagos that, when those of Lagos were using the word "Inago" as their name, and as the name of the language they spoke, they of the French land too adopted the same name; being from the same place. What brought a sudden difference between the two groups of people were the acts of the Governments.

According to the final result of the Berlin Conference of 1885, the whole of Dahomey and districts were assigned to the French Government, and the Cameroons, being first reached by the firm of G.L. Gaiser before any other European, was given to the Germans through the influence of that firm. It was in the same Conference that the whole of Nigeria was allotted to the British Government for being the first to plant its flag at Badagry in 1843, through the advice of Rev. Thomas Birch freeman, the first Methodist Minister to visit Badagry, Abeokuta, and Dahomey in1842 and 1843 respectively. Consequently, in 1893, the French Government declared a Protectorate over Dahomey; and unfortunately the towns of the people of Ketu and those now called "Inagoes", in their territory, ultimately went into French possession.

As the Inagoes of the French territory had thus been separated from those of Lagos, letter No. 115/77, which His Excellency, Sir Alfred C. Moloney, the first Governor of Lagos, wrote on the 23rd of May, 1888, to Alaafin Adeyemi 1, begging the latter for permission to include Lagos in the catalogue of the Yoruba towns as the fourth corner of the whole Yoruba country in place of Ketu, had no effect on them as it had on those of Lagos. Thus, when the people of Lagos became Yorubas, their kinsmen in the French territory, being unaffected by the change brought about by Governor Moloney's letter, continued to bear their old common name of "Inagoes", which up till date have not given up.

EARLY TRADERS AND OUR PEOPLE

When the British Government stopped the sinful slave trade to a reasonable extent, they did not fail to replace it by a more equally lucrative trade, one of whose articles was "Coral Bead", to which more attention was paid by the Syrians and Lebanese than any other traders of our country then. For this reason, our people wishing to call those Syrians and Lebanese by the name of the trade properly, they used to call the Syrians and Lebanese "Kora-a", throughout our country till this day.

The idea of our people calling foreign firms by the names of their trade or trademarks was not peculiar to the Syrians and Lebanese alone. In those days, owing to the incapability of our people to pronounce the names of the various firms trading in our country properly, they used to call them by the names of their trademarks; and others by mere description of their countries. Thus the firm of P.Z. which has Palm Tree as its trade mark was called "Alagbon", or "Oyinbo Alagbon". The firm of Gottschalk, having human palm as its trade mark was called, "Olowo, or Oyinbo Olowo"; and the French Company, which belongs to the Europeans other than the British, under whose flag we are, was called "Oyinbo Ajeji", i.e., "A foreign firm" different from those with whom we have been dealing. Advance in our education has put a stop to our people calling these firms by their old names again.

Apart from the various names already considered above, there is yet one which is more identical to the word "Yoruba" in its deridingly nature from origin than any other. That name is "Kobo-kobo" which the people who are called Yorubas often use for anybody who does not speak the same language they speak. The only people excluded from this are the Northerners.

The word "Kobo-kobo" first came into use when the easterners came to our part of the country, and had not understood our language properly. When they went to the market and asked for something edible, which were priced at 1d. each, the sellers told them that each was "Kobo". Next, they pointed to another group of food so as to know their prices. In reply, the seller said they were all "Kobo-kobo" each round, i.e. 1d. each.

That day, they bought as much as they liked. Wishing afterwards to buy almost everything cheap as before, the easterners used to bargain nearly everything for a penny (1d) each, by saying "Ko gba kobo-kobo?" meaning, wouldn't you let me pay a penny each?

Seeing that those easterners were annoying them with such vexatious method of bargaining their wares, the sellers used to cast frequent gibes on them by saying "Go out of my sight with your kobokobo talks, because you do not know more than "wouldn't you let me pay a penny each?"

In saying these things, the sellers thought that the easterners' constant bargaining for a penny each was mainly due to their pure lack of understanding of our language. Therefore, whenever they saw those easterners, they used to call them "Kobokobo", and gradually it became an uncalled for general name for easterners amongst us.

In course of time, this name became not a little scornful and offensive one to an easterner some years ago, so much so that he had to take days in writing very seriously in one of the highly recognized dailies of our country against the wrong idea of calling them "Kobokobo", because it is a name which has no origin with them at all.

Of all the various names that have been considered, no other one can compare fairly well in its deridingly nature with the word or name "Yoruba", as the word "Kobokobo", which is often refused by the people to whom it is constantly applied. It is, therefore, very alarming to see how thousands of people incessantly make wrong use of this questionable name as if it were the true original name of our race. Some writers even go so far as far as to call Yoruba, the language of Oodua, the progenitor of our whole race; but it seems a pity that the argument of those historians as well as that of their enthusiastic admirers for this misleading assertion is, chiefly based on nothing else than the fact that, we all can easily understand ourselves in speeches.

ORIGIN OF THE WORD YORUBA

Before the origin of the word Yoruba can be fairly known, it will have to be studied in the following three aspects – (1) As an opprobrious name; (2) as a means of helping the early missionaries in their efforts of translating the Holy Bible into our language, and in extending their mission field; and (3) as a means of extending the political territory of the early Government of Lagos.

A) Yoruba as an Opprobrious Name

History reveals that long ago, the dealings of the Oyos with the northern peoples of Nigeria were so long and much that, many writers afterwards assumed that the Hausas and the Yorubas hailed from the same family circle. Some writers even say that the Yorubas were originally the children of one of the seven illegitimate children, supposed to have been born by a certain Queen in Hausa-land. For this reason, they believe that the Yorubas came directly from Hausa land to settle first at Ile-Ife, from where they scattered to their present various towns. Nevertheless, history depicts well that of all the children of Oodua, the Oyos were the first to bear the name "Yoruba". The reason for this is contained in the fact that, in ancient times, there was a big and flourishing market at a place very much near, if not at the exact place now called Bussa. It was a notable market town which the Rev. S. Johnson, the writer of "The History of the Yorubas", called Ogodo, where he declared, Lanloke, an Oyo man, was chief.

Though this market was for both the Oyos and the Northerners, yet, the population of the former preponderated that of the latter there because nearly all the children of influential Oyo Chiefs resided there permanently for the purpose of trade.

As was the custom of those dark days, the chief article of their trade was mainly human traffic. The reason why slave trade was much more indulged in than any other article was the fact that, from time immemorial, there had been a great trade intercourse between the Hausas and the people of North-west Africa; and the bulk of their trade was mostly in slave trade. Consequently, in order to meet the constant demands of the people of North Africa in slaves, the Hausas and the Oyos invented various methods of getting slaves.

It was easy for them to do so because long before the Arabs and the Europeans started slave trade in Africa, slave trade had been going on steadily among the very indigenous Africans themselves.

At that time, the Fulani were mere subordinate entities to the Hausas. Consequently, the latter used to sell the former into slavery at regular intervals at will with impunity. It was after Usuman dan Fodio's return from Mecca in 1802, that the Fulani and Hausa Muslim converts were saved by him from being further enslaved.

In those dark days, slavery system was so deep-rooted among the black people that they did not regard it a sin to enslave even their own children in one form or another whenever they were in need of money. The worst type of slavery was the one in which a man or woman had to give his or her only child away in exchange for the money received from another person. The reason why it was perhaps the worst from of slavery was that, in most cases, many of such parents used to fail entirely to redeem their children. That was why this type of slavery was one of the constant, or unfailing ways through which the ancient slave-dealers used to get their wares to North Africa.

This latter type of slavery was the one which was known as "Iwofa System" in our pert of the country of Nigeria; but among the people of Northern Nigeria, it was known as a real form of slavery, in just the same way as the Europeans knew it to be. Nevertheless, there was one unique aspect of the system, and that is, there was chance for any parent to come and redeem his child whenever he got the money for which he had given his child away, but failing to get the money refunded would make the child become a perpetual and lost slave.

As "Iwofa System" was regarded as a mere inevitable inconvenience, but not as an actual form of slavery in the now called Yoruba country, the people, from whom money had been obtained used to allow grown-up people who had enslaved themselves to the others to sleep in their own homes and come to work in the farms of their owners; but no money-giver would allow any unmarried young man or girl, given to him or her for the money he lent out, to sleep for a day in his or her parent's house without any special reason, strongly supported by the lender's approval. On account of this coercive treatment, many a young man was known to have run away to another far places, in order to be out of reach of both his parents and his oppressive master.

In short, the system of slavery in the actual form was in real operation among the people of Northern Nigeria until Lord F.D. Lugard, as the first High Commissioner of Northern Nigeria, made an order, stating that any child born anywhere in the whole of Northern Nigeria as from the 1st of April, 1901, became free-born whom anybody had the right of making or calling a slave for ever as from that date. The order went on further to say that anybody who happened to sin against that enactment would be seriously dealt with by the Government. Further still, it said that all people who were up to that time known and called slaves in the houses of their respective owners should remain to be so known and treated indefinitely; but any slave who happened o escape from the custody of his, or her master must not for any earthly reason be sought for by his, or her owner. It was still strictly expressed that anybody who willfully disobeyed the order would be severely punished by law.

History reveals that at the time, when such an order had not been made and enforced, a slave, previously sold by his parents curiously found his way out of his master's custody owing, principally to the constant ill-treatment he daily received from his master. In order that he might be able to leave that area entirely, he made his way to the direction of the big market, already referred to as once existing between the Oyos and the Northerners. When he reached that market, he met some Oyo traders. After their warm exchange of greetings, they found out where he was coming from and where he was going alone at that time. After he had given suitable answers to their questions, they gladly gave him plenty of food. Nevertheless, to his utter amazement, no sooner had he stopped eating than he saw some stalwart men with a very strong and moderately large top, round which a stout cord was tied. As soon as they came, they arrested him and threw the top into his mouth before the two arms of the cord, tied round the top were passed to the back of his head, where they were tightly tied together at his occiput. Next, they put him in the room, looking towards the place where they were sitting. That room was covered with a fibre mat. It was so disjointly woven that anybody sitting in the room could clearly see, and distinctly hear anybody talking where the Oyos were.

Very surprisingly, it was not long after they did these things before a horse-rider came in search of this slave. On his first coming in contact with the Oyo traders, he gave them necessary salutation before he told them that he came to them in search of a run-away slave. He told them that those who saw the slave when he was running away made him to understand that he took the way leading from their place to that big market. Therefore, he said that he would feel very much grateful if they could tell him whether the slave had been there, and further, if they would please direct him to where he could easily retrieve him.

In reply, the Oyos said that, truly speaking, the young man came to meet them in the market. He spent some hours in resting under the shade of one of the trees there; but unfortunately, just a few minutes before the horse-rider came to them, they saw the young man going that way (pointing to a road).

As the Oyos were yet talking with the horse-rider, one of them, who left them for a short time to fetch something at home was coming back to them. As he was very near to them, one of them suddenly set this deceiving question to him — "Ngbo, ore wa yi ki yoo le ba omo ti o sese kuro nihin?" Meaning, "Don't you think that this our friend can overtake the youngman who has just left here?" As he was perfectly in the know of all the treatments meted to the kept-slave, he promptly replied thus — "Yoo-ba-a, nitoripe ko iti pe ti o kuro nihin". i.e. Surely, he will overtake him because it has not been a long time since he left here.

On hearing this, they all said as follows in unison — "Yara-o ba-a, oun ni nlo un." i.e. Make haste and overtake him, that's he going.

The kept-slave clearly heard everything they said, but could not say a word, either for or against all that they said. Nevertheless, regarding all that the Oyos told him as a gospel truth, the horse-rider implicitly followed the pieces of advice given him by them. Notwithstanding, in vain did he seek for the run-away slave who was yet kept in their custody. He therefore, returned home, as it were, empty handed; but did not fail to report his sad experience at home.

Some days after this very strange incident, the Oyo traders sold the young man to a man, who again re-sold him to another man.

After a few years of this occurrence, the same slave accompanied his new masters to the same market where he was once sold. Fortunately for him at that time, there were in the market, some people from the house of the parents of this slave. When they saw this salve, they managed one way or the other to speak with him. After they had collected all the necessary information they wanted from him, they gladly went home to report to his parents that they had seen him.

On reaching home, those who had seen the slave and had heard the descriptions he had made to them about how they could easily trace him out in the town where he was, told everything to his parents who had since the escape of this slave from his first master's house been wishing to know his whereabouts, in order that they might be able to pay his redemptive money, with a strong view to bringing him back home. They were wishing to do these things at that time because, they had become well-to-do. Therefore, in as much as they had got some of their people to lead them to where their son was, they lost not in arranging for his redemption.

Eventually, the slave came back home to his people. There, he gave his people, every detailed account of how he escaped from his first master's house, and how he was caught and first kindly treated by some Oyo traders before he was kept in a room, with a top in his mouth; and finally how he was re-sold on two different occasion. He also related how he distinctly heard all that happened between the Oyo traders and the horse-man who pursued him to the Oyo settlement in that big market. More especially, he heard audibly when one of the Oyo traders in reply to the question which one of them put to him said, "Yoo-ba-a, nitoripe ko iti pe ti o kuro nihin", and also when they all said to the horse-man thus – "Yara-o-ba-a, oun ni nlo un."

As there were many people where the redeemed slave told the story of his sad past life, the news of what the Oyo traders did to him soon got afloat, and consequently became the property of many people. Therefore, when it was clearly known by many people that it was the Oyos that cunningly caught and sold the slave, and yet, asked the horse-man to make haste and overtake him, that's he going, the Northerners became so angry that they soon became sworn enemies of the Oyos; but unfortunately for them at that time, the Oyos and their allies were more powerful than either the Fulani or the Hausas, who were then disunited and weak under their sectional Kings. It was the disunity of the Hausas that made the numerically fewer Fulani to conquer them under the leadership of Usuman dan Fodio from 1804 to 1808.

In gaining this sweeping victory first, over the King of Gobir, and secondly over the whole Hausa States. Usuman dan Fodio had the assistance of some sub-Hausa and Fulani Muslim leaders who carried their flags to him for blessing against their unbelieving neighbours. Those leaders were then known and called "Standard-bearers". After the full conquest of the whole North, he gave them the name "Emirs", and in 1808, he made his son Bello, the first Sultan of Sokoto over them all, while he himself continued preaching about.

Nevertheless, there were three tribes that were strongly opposed to the Fulani incursions. They were the Kanuris in the east, the Plateau Hill tribes and the Yorubas in the South. The following extract from Iwe Kika Ekerin lie de Yoruba, page 49, and paragraph 1, serves as an example of the true position of things between the Fulani and the Yorubas then – "A ni a ri awon ti awon Filani ima beru ti nwon ko si je kada won ko; ninu awon naa ti o se oloruko ni ile Ijoba Yoruba." (Meaning, There is a certain body of people whom the Fulani owed in great awe, and dared not go to oppose; famous among such were people of the Yoruba Kingdom).

To support this point further, the words of another writer, as contained in The History of the Yorubas, page 217, and a portion of paragraph 1, are quoted as follows – "Prince Amodo was one of the grand children of Ajampati, the twin brother of Ajagbo. He came to the throne at the time when the Kingdom was disturbed by anarchy and confusion. The Fulanis having an eye on the capital of Yoruba land, but not being confident enough to make an attack on the city whilst there were so many powerful chiefs in the land, who might suddenly return to their allegiance, were using prudence and astuteness to spread disaffection."

It may be remarked here that not only were the Hausa and Fulani using prudence and astuteness to spread disaffection, but were also actually stunting the Oyos in their common market place with such spiteful expressions as the following – "Yoo-ba-a, or Yara-o-ba-a, or people with many evasive words are coming, beware of them."

For this reason, the Oyos often quarreled with them. One of the chief things that made the Oyos feel annoyed with them was the sharp line of distinction which they used to make between those who had various facial tribal marks, and those who had none from among our people. They regarded the former as "Yoo-ba-a, or Yara-o-ba-a, or people with many evasive words, and finally as Yorubas." To the latter, they gave the name of "Be-e-rebe whom they regarded as being more reliable than the former.

After some time of serious quarrelling between the two sections when the Oyos perceived that their opponents could do nothing of importance to them, not only did they allow other people to call them by those opprobrious names, but they themselves took a great pride in being so known and called. They did this in order that they might be able to strike terror into the minds of their opponents.

It must particularly be noted that the pride in this name Yoruba did not stop where mention has just been made above, but in another form, it also gained a great deal of ground among the Oyos of Ibadan sometime ago, when they used to say to a person whom they had cleverly duped or cheated thus – "Ibadan l'omo, o-o mo laipo, Laipo baba Ibadan." Meaning, "It is only Ibadan that you know, but you do not know laipo *(Circumambages)*, the erstwhile progenitor of the Ibadans.

If the merit or demerit of the word "Laipo", is gone into, it will actually be found that no better interpretation could be found for it than Yoruba." It must be at once remarked that this does not in any way mean the people whom we call Yoruba today. It simply means the word "Yoruba", used by anyone to deceive another; and consequently, it does not belong to any particular person. If on the other hand, effort is made to find out the real meaning of the word "Yoruba", it will not, in all probability, be far from "Saying one thing and doing another."

In defence of this name, some people are always in the habit of saying that the word "Yoruba" is quite different from "Yoruba people" in the ways they are used for us today. Nevertheless, so long as the real distinction between the two has not yet been made known to us, the world is yet to receive the unalloyed explanations of those who believe in the distinction between the two. Hereto, our limited knowledge of the whole thing is, that the sum total of the despiteful names of "Yoo-ba-a", and "Yara-o-ba-a" was the root of the tree which produced the name "Yoruba", which first became the name of the Oyos before it came to be the national name of us all through the powerful instrumentality of the earliest representatives of the C.M.S. in our Country.

(B) Yoruba as a Means of Helping the Early Missionaries

The second clear aspect of the word Yoruba as our today common name is that which has to do with the early writing of books translating the Holy Bible into our language, and of extending the C.M.S. Mission Field in our land. In order therefore, to understand these points well, it will be necessary to deal first with "When and Why we all were first known as Yorubas."

As a result of a frantic appealing letter to a Methodist Minister Rev Thomas Dove in Sierra Leone, by an "Aku" Methodist member, who, with some other Egba refugees had since 1839 come to settle with their people at Abeokuta, wrote in the month of January, 1841, as well as that one written on the 2nd of March of the same year by James Ferguson, another Egba refugee, from Badagry to the same Minister, both Methodist and C.M.S. missions began very seriously to make preparations for short visits to Badagry and Abeokuta, where they had heard that God had started His work among the heathens at the hands of their old Aku members.

Three months later, while they were making those preparations, a very different correspondent, Captain Richard Lawrence, R.N., also wrote to Rev Thomas Dove from Whydah, calling his attention to the great need for a missionary at Whydah, if both missionaries and the British Government wanted slave trade be really stamped out of West Africa.

No sooner the news conveyed by Captain Lawrence's letter reached England than Thomas Fowell Buxton's Society, which had since its inauguration in 1839 made it its avowed object to help the Africans in their own land, called a public meeting, which had as its Chairman, the Prince Consort.

The meeting was, in nature, so rousing that several people openly volunteered to come to our country, if the Government could provide all that was necessary for the voyage.

Seeing the eagerness of the people in regard to this matter, the Government promptly agreed to send an expedition in 1841, under the leadership of Captain Trutter and others. As the Niger was the only known most serviceable means of travelling in our land at that time, the expedition was sent to the Niger Coast, which had for a long time before been their object in view to explore.

In order that the expedition might have full strength to work, Government asked C.M.S. Mission to send two of its men, working at Sierra Leone, to accompany the expedition. In addition, the Ibos of Sierra Leone were asked to send a dozen men to accompany the expedition as interpreters.

The two men whom the C.M.S. authorities sent were a linguist, Rev James Fredrick Schon, who had studied both Ibo and Hausa languages in Tripoli, and Samuel Ajayi Crowther, then a tutor at Fourah Bay College, Sierra Leone; but unfortunately, these men reached the Niger in the month of August, when the place was full of mosquito. Consequently, the expedition was so disastrous that within two months of its being in the Niger Coast, not only forty-two of its 164 members died of fever, but only Crowther and the Doctor remained unaffected before John Beecroft, the first British Consul on the West Coast of Africa, came to their aid, at a place very near Jebba. After taking care of the remaining men at Fernando Po, they went to England and Sierra Leone respectively.

After all, the report which Mr Schon sent to the C.M.S. authorities included the following – "The sum total of what we went for was a complete failure, and consequently, if we really want to work on the Niger Coast, the authorities must find an African, capable of holding up the fort of carrying on the Gospel of Christ on the Niger Coast."

As there was no other African more capable then than Crowther could be found to vie with the grave situation, the choice fell on Ajayi Crowther.

Before that time, all the liberated slaves belonging to

our part of the country were known by the name "Akus", or "Okus" as previously explained. As Crowther was a very active and long visioned man, he started to think out what he could do to make him better known and more distinguished than any other of his country people in Sierra Leone. Not very long, the thought of writing a book haunted him. In order to be able to do this effectively, he started to collect material from the elders of his tribe for his two books which he began soon after his name had been submitted for further studies in England, with a view to ordaining him as a future minister for Niger Coast.

As a book without a name will be of little value, Crowther gave his two books in 1842, the names of Yoruba Vocabulary and Yoruba Grammar respectively.

He was able to give those names to his two books because the small town of Oshogun, very near to the town of Iseyin, where he was born in Oyo division, was one of the places where Yoruba was first used as a name; and he, being a boy of about 12 or even more years of age before he was caught and sold into slavery, was able to know "Yoruba" as a name, and, therefore, after consultations with some elders, he applied those names to his books.

In order to make his dreams about Yoruba a realistic one, not only did Crowther continue writing his Yoruba books on board the ship as he was going to England, but even when he was busy studying in Islington College, he did not fail to add the work of the translation of the Holy Bible into Yoruba language to the continuation of the writing of his previously mentioned books.

Seeing the activities of Crowther, other European missionaries like Townsend and Gollmer, began very earnestly to interest themselves in the study and writing of Yoruba Books. Consequently, Mr Gollmer was able to translate a part of the New Testament into Yoruba before they left Sierra Leone in 1845, because at that time, the

Bible was translated into our own language in pieces of Matthew, Mark, Luke John, etc. according to the imperfect alphabet introduced by Crowther.

COMING OF THE MISSIONARIES TO ABEOKUTA

According to the advice of Rev H. Townsend to the authorities of the C.M.S. Mission in 1843, that if they really wanted to work in Abeokuta, they must not send less than six missionaries there at once, the C.M.S. sent Revs H. Townsend, C.A. Gollmer and S.A. Crowther with some six other African workers early in January, 1845 and they reached Badagry on January 17 of that year. But unfortunately, owing to the inter tribal war between Ado and Abeokuta, these missionaries had to stay for eighteen months at Badagry before Townsend and Crowther could reach Abeokuta on the 3rd of August, 1846, leaving Gollmer at Badagry. Thus they then had two centres of work.

In 1848, Rev David Hinderer, one of the German missionaries then in the service of the C.M.S. joined the worker of Abeokuta, where he was stationed at Oshiele. He was at this place till the early part of the month of May, 1851, when he obtained permission from the Egba Chiefs to carry the Gospel of Jesus Christ to Ibadan. His request having been granted, he set out for Ibadan, which he reached on the 16th of May, 1851, after a four day circuitous journey.

During the first five months he spent at Ibadan, he founded a mission station at Ijaye along with that of Ibadan. Owing, however, to lack of assistants, he left for England in the fifth month, and having married Miss Anne Martin early in December 1852, he returned to Ibadan with his wife and Mr Keffer to begin the work in reality.

At this time, not only did he write many books, but he

translated the whole of the Pilgrim's Progress into the language of the people among whom he was working, and consequently, all the vernacular books used at Ibadan then were called Yoruba Books.

Owing to the unfruitfulness of the Missionary work at Badagry, the Mission authorities asked Rev C.A. Gollmer to remove to Lagos in the early part of 1852.

His work in Lagos developed so quickly that he started to write books for the use of his flock too. The people of Lagos having been partially known by the name of Inago through the influence of the immigrants from Brazil, all the vernacular books, used in Lagos though the missionaries called them Yoruba books, were called "Iwe Inago", by the natives.

At that time too, the Egbas would not like to be known or called either Yorubas or Inagoes; and consequently, all the vernacular books used at Abeokuta were called "Iwe Egba", and they used to speak of their language as "Ede Egba" but all the same, the missionaries who knew their ultimate end in view, used to call the newspaper they were writing then by these two names – "Iwe Irohin fun awon Egba ati Yoruba", so that the peoples of Abeokuta and Ibadan might not grudge one another because, although the newspapers were for the three groups into which the controlling centres of work were divided, yet, a true Ibadan man would like to hear that the peoples of Abeokuta, Ijebu or even Ile-Ife were ranked with the Yorubas then.

NECESSITY FOR ONE COMMON BIBLE

In order to make their ideas become a realistic one, the missionaries of the three centres – Lagos, Abeokuta and Ibadan, seeing that the people of Lagos and Abeokuta were unwilling to be called Yorubas as they would like them all be known and called, met together to consider how they could best solve the problem of unifying the dialects of the three groups of people, among whom they were working so as to make Yoruba their common name.

Being told that, originally, all those people were the subjects of the Alaafin of Oyo, and finding Oyo dialect much more pleasing to hear, understand, and much easier to reduce into writing than that of any of the other two, they all agreed to combine the different books of the Bible written in Oyo dialect into one book and call it *Bibeli Mimo li Ede Yoruba.*

The main implied object of doing that was, instead of urging those people to adopt Yoruba as a common name, the towns or countries where that Bible was read, and continued to be read would automatically become Yoruba towns, or countries respectively. In like manner, the people reading that Bible would become Yorubas. This was the way we all became Yorubas unawares.

This was not the only arrangement they made, but they went further still to claim the following as being Yoruba towns from the fact that they all could unhesitatingly trace their origin from Ile-Ife – the Egbados, Barapas, Yorubas, Egbas, Ijebus, Ifes, Ondos, Ijeshas, Ekitis, Igbominas, Bunus, Benins with their dependencies, Sekiris, Ijos, Aticos, Akokos, Idowanis, and Owos. The full account of this point will be dealt with again in this history.

No sooner had they concluded these arrangements than they began to translate the Bible in the way they thought would best serve their purpose; but unfortunately, all their efforts proved abortive. As a proof, vide The History of the Yorubas, page 23, paragraph 2 where it reads thus, "After several fruitless efforts had been made either to invent new characters or adopt the Arabic which was already known to Moslem Yorubas, the Roman character was naturally adopted, not only because it would obviate the difficulties that must necessarily arise if missionaries were first to learn strange characters before they could undertake scholastic and evangelistic work..."

In order to make their efforts of greater effect than before, the authorities of the C.M.S. Mission called in, the assistance of three Philological Doctors who were Professor Lee of Cambridge, Mr Norries of London, and Professor Lepsius of Berlin, to whom was given the duty of establishing a complete form of alphabetic system to which all hitherto unwritten languages could be adapted.

Having therefore, got what they really wanted, the C.M.S. adopted the standardized alphabetic system of those Doctors in the year 1856. Their translated works were then done under this system; and it was then that they began by degrees to put an end to the terms "Iwe Inago, Ede Inago", "Iwe Egba and "Ede Egba", respectively.

As a proof of this, vide "The History of the Yorubas, page 24, and a portion of paragraph 1", where it reads thus – "This was adopted by the C.M.S. in 1856, former translations had to be translated under certain fixed rules".

By this method, the word "Yoruba", was begun to be used gradually as the common name of the various tribes among whom the Gospel was being preached in our land. Eventually, people took the name so without resistance, because what was then uppermost in the mind of every believer was the salvation of his own soul; and therefore, only very few people cared for correct or incorrect history or our land then.

Nevertheless, to show further that originally, Yoruba was not our common national or racial name, read below a portion of what Bishop I. Oluwole said in the paper read by him at the S.M.S. Conference of workers, held at Lagos from February 3rd to 9th, 1896 running thus – "The people whom we, for the sake of convenience now call Yorubas are the Yorubas proper, the Egbas, the Ijebus, the Ekitis, etc,"

In like manner, in the paper read by him at the C.M.S. Conference of Clergymen, held at Ibadan from January 23rd to 26th, 1899, Bishop C. Phillips, late of Ondo, and the revered father of Bishop S.C. Phillips, the Vicar-General, now resident at Osogbo, read among many other things the following – "This Mission has not yet made good its claim to the title of 'Yoruba Mission' by which it is designated. The name Yoruba, (for want of a more comprehensive term and for the convenience of the civilized world) is now applied to a country which extends from the Borgu kingdom on the north, to the Bight of Benin on the south, and from the Dahomean territory on the west, to the river Niger on the east."

(C) Yoruba As A Means Of Helping Governor Moloney's Territorial Expansion

Replying on what he had gleaned from both the early missionaries and the officials before him in office, His Excellency, Sir Alfred C. Moloney, C.M.G., made, when he came to office as the first Governor of Lagos, the unification of the Yorubas, one of his chief public objects. His unrevealed aim in this was, to cement more firmly the half buried matter, previously started by the missionaries. He continued doing this gradually until 23rd May, 1888, when he was strongly moved to write the letter, reading as seen below, to King Adeyemi 1, the Alaafin of Oyo –

Government House, Lagos,
May 23rd, 1888
No. 115/77

"King – I received with much pleasure your letter of the 20th February last, and beg to thank you for the present of two cloths of the country, any manufacture of which interests me indeed.

"2. To show my esteem to you and my appreciation of the position you occupy I have asked the Revd S. Johnson, who returns to his ministerial duties to salute you and your people with my compliments and respect, and to wish well to you and yours.

"3. As you know, and every Yoruba knows, people to the West and North are not Yorubas; they differ in feelings and object from Yorubas. You will have doubtless learnt I always aim at making all Yoruba speaking peoples one in heart as they are in tongue.

"4. Towards such unity I attach importance to a definite and permanent understanding between these Yoruba speaking peoples, and this Colony which is mainly inhabited by Yorubas. And where should I look first sympathy and support but to Adeyemi, the Alaafin of Oyo, the titular king of all Yorubas?

"5. Between you and the Governor of the Queen's Colony of Lagos there should be ever friendship, goodwill which no foreign interference should be allowed to influence or disturb.

"6. Yorubaland was comprised traditionally as regards its corners a few years ago of Yoruba proper, Egba, Ketu and Ijebu. Where is Ketu now? And from what direction was it destroyed?

"7. Without the entertainment of the least desire to meddle with the Government of such Kingdoms as Yoruba, Egba, Ijebu and with the assurance that not one yard of land is coveted by me, in feeling and for Yoruba union, I desire that Lagos take the place of Ketu as the fourth corner.

"8. If the accompanying document be agreeable to you

and embodies your wishes, sign and return it to me. If your relations with country to the north of yours be such as to admit of your persuading them what is to their interest, I would be glad to find you can get its people to sign a paper similar to the one I proposed to yourself *(i.e. peoples to the West and North)*... I venture to send you five pounds as a small present; wishing you and all your people every good wish.

> "I am, King,
> Your good friend,
> *(Sgd)* Alfred C. Moloney,
> Governor."

Before closing this chapter, it will perhaps be a bit helpful if the following points are taken notice of –

1) If originally we all were Yorubas under the headship of the Alaafin of Oyo, from whom those that Governor Moloney wanted to unite into a nation had long severed their connection for one reason or another, the same Alaafin should not have been the authority to depend on for the reunion of his long scattered subjects.

2) If really, the reunion of the Yorubas, and not just to make a Yoruba nation was the main aim of that letter, Governor Moloney should have used his influence with Captain (afterwards Lord Lugard) and other influential Europeans of the north to transfer the Ilorin and the Igbomina Yorubas to his sphere of influence in the south quite a long time ago.

3) If originally, we all were Yorubas under the rule of the Alaafin, it would have been the duty of the Governor merely, to settle the misunderstanding which had long disunited the various tribes of the people who should have already known themselves as Yoruba before that time, instead of persuading them to become Yorubas through

the signing of some papers, which were not shown to the people mostly concerned.

4) If Alaafin had power over Lagos then, not only should we have known the reply he gave to the Governor on the Lagos question, but the Lagos Chiefs should have known why and when they became the fourth corner of the Yoruba Kingdom in place of Ketu, just as they knew the time their own became a British Colony in 1862, and why?

5) If, truly we all were originally Yorubas, the Governor himself would not have written thus – "Without the entertainment of the least desire to meddle with the Governments of such Kingdoms as Yorubas, Egba, Ijebu."

To be sure that Lagos Government wanted extension at that time, *vide*, "The History of Nigeria", by A.C. Burns, page 145, paragraph 2, read thus – "The Colony of Lagos was now firmly established. Its boundaries had been extended to the east and west and in the Yoruba country, its influence was steadily growing."

CROWTHER'S FINAL CONTRIBUTION TO THE FURTHERANCE OF YORUBA

In trying to force the name "Yoruba" on us all the more, the Rev, (afterwards) Bishop S.A. Crowther was reported to have said in his letter to Thomas J. Hutchinson Esq., Her Britannic Majesty Consul for the Bight of Biafra and the Island of Fernando Po as published in a book, entitled "Impressions of Western Africa", the following among many other things – "This part of the country of which Lagos in the Bight of Benin, is the Seaport, is generally known as the Yoruba country, extending from the Bight to within two or three days' journey to the banks of the Niger. This country comprises many tribes, governed by their own Chiefs and having their own laws. At one time, they were tributaries to one Sovereign, the King of Yoruba, including Benin on the East, and Dahomey on the West, but are now independent.

If the descriptions made by Bishop Crowther are carefully and closely followed along with other facts already told, it will be seen that the area described by him did not merely mean that part of the whole country directly ruled over by the Alaafin of Oyo, as they were meant to convey, on the ground that Alaafin's people were the first to be known as Yoruba; but the descriptions actually embraced the whole area covered by the new Yoruba country, made by the missionaries. If the latter was the thought of the respected Bishop, then it will be clear to the readers that the name "Yoruba" was forced on us for the following reasons –

1) In the whole of our country, the Oyos were the first to whom the word "Yoruba" was scornfully applied.

2) The Benin and the Lagos peoples were never once before under either the direct or indirect rule of the Alaafin of Oyo.

3) It was only the Ooni of Ife who could authoritatively claim that right over the whole country then, because he was the original accredited father and head of all the other Obas of our country, including Alaafin himself.

It will be interesting to know that, until the occupation of the whole of our land by the British, the Oba of Benin still acknowledged the suzerainty of the Ooni of Ife. It must not also be forgotten that until the occupation of Lagos by the same British, Lagos was one of the tributaries of Benin.

Ooni was the head of the whole country now called Yoruba country, and to him were the other Chiefs tributaries when the country had not been known as Yoruba country, but Ife Empire. The efforts of some people to make another man usurp his position as head of our whole country has largely drifted many people from speaking facts about the true origin of the Yorubas.

WERE THE IFES, EGBAS, IJEBUS, EKITIS AND ONDOS YORUBAS ORIGINALLY?

The above question may certainly sound very queer to many readers who have hitherto regarded the above mentioned tribes, not only as common or improper, but salmon pure Yorubas proper. It may perhaps be so strange to many that they will not like to read or even hear of it; but it should be noted that, it will pay us all much better to read this portion of the history patiently and very carefully than to put it aside. It is only by patient and sober reading of it that what the authorities have got to tell us can really be grasped. On the other hand, it is by reading the accounts of the authorities that we can be able to judge aright.

Below will be found a few of the statements of the authorities –

1) When the Ibadans were eventually hermetically hemmed in on all sides by their enemies during the long and devastating Kiriji War, it strongly obliged the Rev. D. Hinderer in his sheer sympathy for the Ibadans, amongst whom he had laboured for clear 17 years, to write a very thought provoking letter to the Christian representatives of all the various tribes of our land then resident in Lagos.

As a result of that letter, a meeting of those Christians, presided over by the late Rev. (afterwards) Bishop James Johnson was held at Breadfruit Parsonage, Lagos, on the 7th of December, 1882.

The following is the resolution passed in that memorable meeting – "At a meeting of the representative elders of the different tribes, Yorubas, Egbas, Ijebus, Ifes, Ijeshas, and Ondos, held at Breadfruit Parsonage on the 7th December, 1882, in reference to the long standing warfare in the interior, from which both the interior countries and Lagos have suffered, the following resolution was after a full consideration of the subject unanimously adopted…"

2) The Ifes were the original founders and real owners of the town of Ibadan before the Oyos, who rebelled under the leadership of Opele, the Baale of Gbogun, against the Alaafin, and beheaded his brother, came to take refuge under the Ife and Ijebu Confederate armies at Ibadan. After remaining with the Ifes and Ijebus for some years, they cunningly rose up against their benefactors and killed thousands of them in cold blood. After Maye, the Ife generalissimo had been killed, Laboside, whose father was an Ife too, and whose mother was an Oyo, became the head of the Oyos of Ibadan. If, therefore, the Ifes were Yorubas originally, Rev. S. Johnson would not have on page 238, and section 3 of "The History of the Yorubas", as follows – "How Ibadan Finally Became A Yoruba Town."

3) Again, if the Ifes were originally Yorubas, it would not have been possible for an Ooni of Ife to be a Yoruba man, only on his mother's side. For the proof of this, *vide* "The History of the Yorubas", page 230, paragraph 3, reading thus – "A pretext was soon found again for murdering the well disposed Owoni. Adegunle succeeded to the throne; he was partly of Yoruba descent on the mother's side, and hence was the benefactor of the Oyos all his days."

4) When the town of Abeokuta was about to be founded , an important meeting was held by the Egba War Chiefs. The account of the meeting was afterwards given in the following words – "It came to pass after this war, Lamodi, an Igbein man–the general of all Egbas, Sodeke, his next man in command, with Degesi–the Seriki, an Ijeun man, held a meeting at which they resolved that, it as high time that they should stop fighting against the Ijebus, Ifes, and the Yorubas, and that they should go and found a

105

settlement of their own, so that their children might not be utterly destroyed."

Here again, it is obviously seen that Yorubas were cleanly and separately mentioned from both Ifes and Ijebus.

5) On page 75, and paragraphs, 1 and 2 of Iwe Kika Ekerin Li Ede Yoruba, are found the following passages – "During the time that Yorubaland was as it was previously described, it would appear that from heaven came naturally, upon the whole Yorubaland, a certain very dreadful thing, brought into Yorubaland by the various kinds of unrest from among those that were forced into the Yoruba group. In addition, their want of peace was much greater than that of the Yorubas Proper."

"It seems that not a single Yoruba slave ever reached Sierra Leone until 1818 or 1820 A.D. It was among the Egba and the Ijebu slaves and those of other towns already mentioned, that Rev. W. Johnson came to labour in Sierra Leone, and were found to be dull of understanding."

YORUBAS PROPER

As it has been previously stated, not only the Oyos today, but the Egbas, Ijebus, Ifes, Ekitis, Ondos, Owos and Aworis are known and called Yorubas Proper.

It always gives one a great amusement on the one hand, and a deep sorrow of heart, on the other hand, when these people are seen making glory in being so called, apart from calling themselves Yorubas Proper.

Their main reasons for doing this are –

(1) They believe that so long as they all can speak to the clear understanding of one another, they all are Yorubas Proper. If this statement is upheld by everybody, it will be a wonder who will be the "Improper Yorubas", and that

will be the criterion upon which they are so considered.

For instance, when we say "Little Britain", we mean the cradle of the British Empire; and by this, we refer to the British Isles, which include England, Scotland, Ireland and Wales. When on the other hand, we say "Great Britain", we mean the whole British Commonwealth of Nations, in which Nigeria is a part. That is why it is often spoken of as an Empire on which the sun never sets.

In the like manner, so long as we have Yorubas Proper, it is imperatively essential that we should know which of our tribes are "Improper Yorubas," and why they are so known and called.

(2) Our people have allowed themselves to be called Yorubas and Yorubas Proper, and even proudly call themselves so because, they think that Oodua, their accredited progenitor was really the founder of the Yoruba, and not of Ife nation. Against this notion, it may be said that if Oodua, who lived, reigned and died at Ile-Ife was the founder of the Yoruba kingdom, and not of Ife nation, naturally, not only Yoruba, but also the term Yoruba Proper should have originated from Ile-Ife, and with the Ifes instead of from Oyo, and with the Oyos, who are but a part of the Ife race.

It will be remembered that it has previously been said that, of all Oodua's children, the Oyos were the first to be known and called "Yorubas", and when the term "Yorubas" was given to us all the Oyos, who had been bearing the name were accorded the honour of being known and called "Yorubas Proper."

EVEN THE OYOS WERE NOT ORIGINALLY YORUBAS

Certainly, it will not in any way be a little wonder to many to learn that not only were we not known and called Yorubas, but even the Oyos were not originally known and called Yorubas. The original common name for all the children of Oodua was "Ifes". The distinguishing name which each tribe bears today does not in any way make its people free from being known and called Ifes still, because each tribe is to Ile-Ife what each quarter of a town in our land is to that town; or in England, what each borough is to the Capital. For example, the whole people of Abeokuta are known as the Egbas, and yet, they are divided into Ake, Owu, Gbagura, Ikija, Iporo, etc., respectively. As it is at Abeokuta, so also it is with all the towns and countries of the world.

The original local name of the Oyos immediately they left Ile-Ife was Oyos and not Yorubas or Yorubas Proper, as they afterwards acme to be known. For this reason, the other tribes used to speak of them merely as the Oyos and not as Yorubas. This custom gained so much ground among the Ijebus that they used to call the day preceding every Ejirin Market Day, the "Oyo Market Day" (Ojo-Oja-Oyo). This day was so named, because it was the day on which the Ibadans, who were then known and called Oyos used to stay and sell some of their wares *(especially native black soap)* at Ijebu-Ode before proceeding to Ejirin. This custom was still in vogue until increase in motor traffic put an end to it some years ago.

Unlike any other son of Oodua, Oloyo arrived at the decision of calling his carved town Oyo, because of the strong injunction which his father Oodua gave him before he left Ile-Ife.

Being a man accidentally born in the palace, very much against the Ife ancient standing rule, his father Oodua gave him a horse to ride on leaving Ile-Ife, and was asked to settle nowhere else until he reached a place where the foot of his horse would slip. The word slip, in our language means "Yo". Consequently, Oyos implies one, who slips. In as much as Oloyo, whose real name was "Omolaofin" was not travelling alone, the name Oyo was collectively applied to his people and himself.

The instruction of settling nowhere else but wherever the foot of his horse slipped given to Omolaofin, now pronounced "Alaafin", was to show to him perpetually that he slipped into the midst of his brethren in a cunning way; and hence the Oyos are from time immemorial known as "slippery customers".

To prove this point more satisfactorily, the following passages are quoted – (i) On page 13, and paragraph 8, of the History of the Yorubas, we read, "Modakeke, a large and growing town, peopled by Oyos of the Ekun Osi, has sprung up in the Ife district just beyond the borders of the Ibolos". (ii) A part of paragraph 9 of the same book reads, "But Ibadan, which was originally an Egba village, then the military station of the Confederate army which destroyed the City of Owu, and the Egba villages, and afterwards a settled Oyo town." (iii) On page 14, paragraph 2, we read "Ijaye, formerly an Egba town became peopled by the Oyos, chiefly from Ekun Osi (Ikoyi districts)" (iv) Page 223, paragraph 1,of the same book reads "We have seen above *(Chapter vii)* that after the fall of Owu, and the punishment inflicted upon some Egba towns for secretly befriending the beleaguered City, the Camp at Idi Ogugun broke up and the leading Ife and Ijebu generals returned home to their respective masters, but the rest of the allied armies with the Oyo refugees were invited by the Ijebus to Ipara, a town of Ijebu-Remo." (v) Paragraph 6 of the same page reads. "Rich with the booty of these expeditions, and finding no fresh fields of operation for their arms, they decide to disband the army. The Ijebu war chiefs returned home, and the Ifes set out to return by way of Oorun – the Oyos who had nowhere to go accompanied them. There were thousands of Oyos already in Ife districts." (vi) On page 224, from the last line to the beginning of page 225, we read, "Next to him (Maye of Ife) was Laboside, also an Ife, but through his mother, of Oyo descent." (vii) On page 490of the same book, we read "The following letter addressed to some gentleman at Lagos will show how strained the Ibadans now were from the use of the rifles against them.

To I.H. Willoughby Esq. (2) D.C. Taiwo Esq. (3) Sumonu Animasawun Esq. (4) Shitta Esq. And all Lagos Oyos or Yorubas"

A portion of paragraph 2 of page 525 of the same book reads – "He stated (as we have learnt above), that they were originally refugees from the ancient Oyo Province, who escaped South when the Fulanis became masters of the country. They were well received at first at Ife, and treated with much sympathy and cordiality, but the turning point of the cordial relations came when Maye, the Ife general was expelled from Ibadan and the Oyos gained the ascendancy in that town. Then the systematic method of cruelty began to be practiced on the Oyos of the City of Ife."

ANCIENT YORUBA COUNTRY AND ITS EXTENT

The Yoruba country as people know and call our country today chiefly consists of the following – Oyo, Ibadan, Abeokuta, Ile-Ife, Ijebu, Ijesha, Ondo, Ekiti, and Awori, with all their respective districts.

In order to throw some light on this seemingly dark matter, it is thought requisite to let the readers know that the first Yoruba country over which the Alaafin of Oyo was the supreme head was, originally divided into two main groups called "Ekun Otun, *(right side)* and Ekun Osi, *(left side)* respectively. Later on, perhaps for administrative purposes, these two groups were regrouped into the following four sections – (1) Ekun Otun (2) Ekun Osi (3) Ibolo and (4) Epo. Vide Iwe Kika Ekerin Li Ede Yoruba, page 57.

These were the towns of the right side – Oyo, Kisi, Gboho, Popo, Dada-Adeyi, Gbogun, Igbeti, Kusu, Iya-Olugbokun, Oje, Agbonle, Kobaye, Erubu, Agbagi, Babo, Otefon, Edogun, Pamumo, Ikoyi, Soundo, Fedegbe, Ogbomojugun, Ile-Alapa, Gogo, Esinole, Ogbomoso, Eso-okun, Gbodo, Akese, Okuta, Imo-kogboro-anko, Eruwa, Isaba-para, Sinrinkun, Iwo-Ohele, Oke-omo, Igbede, Abe, Ogidi-apasa, Igbonjo, Ago, Iyelu, Obate, Saki, Sabigana, Ijana.

The towns of the left hand were – Ejigbo, Ikoyi-Odan, Iwo, Gudugbu, Ile-Tela, Ile-Ogo, Ile-Obe, Iran, Ikoko, Itosi, Iware, Lakale, Lakade, Ika-odan, Ofa-Ojoku, Iragbiji, Enu-Ikirun, Agba-Ire, Ilobu, Ede, Ijaye, Ijebu, Ado, Ota, Dahomi, Bariba, Ijosa, Efon, Igbomina and also other towns.

THE KINGLETS AND THE PROVINCES OF ANCIENT YORUBA COUNTRY

It is the strongly common belief of thousands of people that at a certain period, all the Obas of our land were under the headship of the Alaafin of Oyo. Nevertheless, as far as it is known, this statement seems to be far from being correct.

As previously stated, the Yoruba country was eventually divided into four provinces of (a) Ekun Otun, (b) Ekun Osi, (c) Ibolo and (d) Epo respectively.

The kinglets in the Ekun-Otun were – Sabigana of Igana, Oniware of Iware, Alasia of Asia, Onjo of Oke'ho.

Bagijan of Igijan, Okere of Saki, Alapata of Ibode, Ona-Onibode, of Igboho, Erinpo of Ipapo, Ikihisi of Kihisi,

Aseyin of Iseyin, Alado of Ado, Eleruwa of Eruwa and Oloje of Oje.

In the Ekun Osi were: Onikoyi of Ikoyi, Olugbon of Igbon, Aresa of Iresa, the Ompetu of Ijeru and Olofa of Ofa.

In the Ibolo Province were – The Akirun of Ikirun, Olobu of Ilobu, Timi of Ede, the Ataoja of Osogbo, and Adimula of Ife-Odan.

In the Epo Province were – The Oluiwo of Iwo, and Ondese of Idese.

Of these vassal kings, the Onikoyi, Olugbon, the Aresa, and the Timi were the most ancient. Owing however, to the subsequent wave of Fulani invasion, the first three of these having been swept away, their titles remain only in name now. The Onikoyi has a quarter at Ibadan, but the majority of the Ikoyi people being at Ogbomoso, the family is still extant and the title kept up.

Olugbon is now subject to the Baale of Ogbomoso, and Aresa, to the Emir of Ilorin.

It is particularly worthy of notice here that all the important towns of our whole country such as Lagos, Abeokuta, Ibadan, Ile-Ife, Ijebu, Ilesa, Ondo and Ekiti as well as Awori towns, forming our present day Yoruba country, Ijebu is the only one found in the catalogue of the towns of the ancient Yoruba Country. In the first place, its inclusion in such a list might mean that, in the Oyo area, there was a small town of the same name. otherwise, it will in the second place mean that the inclusion of Ijebu in such a list might spell a pure accident; because it has been previously proved in several places how, not only were our Obas not once under the headship of the Alaafin of Oyo, as they were under the Ooni of Ife, but also that the Ibadans, who claim to be Yorubas Proper today, were not then in the catalogue of Alaafin's Yoruba country.

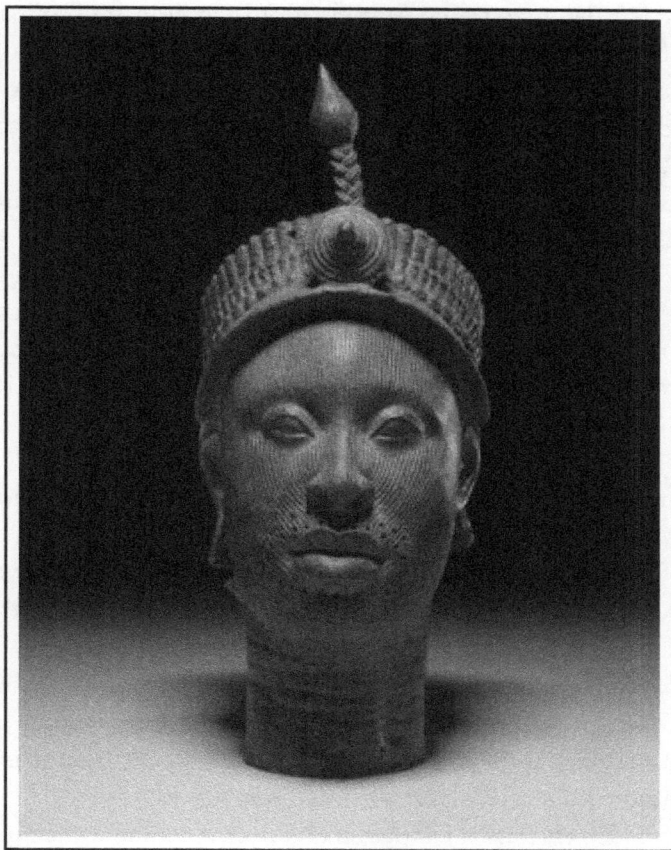

Olokun was one of Oodua's many wives. The long marks on her face were not made with a knife, but with some pieces of broken brooms covered with cotton dipped into a certain fluid mixture of potash and lime juice

WHY AND WHEN OYOS CAME TO IBADAN

It is an undeniable fact that, right from the time that Alaafin had left Ile-Ife to found Oyo kingdom according to Oodua's definite instructions, he was head and overlord of the whole people of the first known Yoruba country. But towards the close of the 18th century, and very early part of the 19th century, some of his dissatisfied subjects began to raise up serious instructions against him, long before the Fulani invasion of the country.

In 1824 and 1825, when Commander Clapperton and his servant Richard Lander visited ancient Oyo, Alaafin's kingdom had not yet been invaded by the Fulani, whom Afonja, the governor of Ilorin invited to his town in 1810, in order to help him against Alaafin his overlord.

According to the account given by Richard Lander during his third visit to the Niger, the invasion of Alaafin's kingdom by the Fulani of Ilorin did not start till 1826 or 1827, when Afonja had no more strong men of his own, and he himself became very old and weak; whereas, the first insurrection, captained by Opele, the Baale of Gbogun, against was much earlier than that of 1804, when Afonja and Alaafin Awole had a very serious alteration, consequent upon which the former invited the Fulani and Hausa into our country as stated above.

This rebellion of Opele had so far reaching effects on the Alaafin that, not only were his wives and messengers checked from doing violence to, and taking properties of the others as freely as before, but Alaafin himself was so reduced down that Opele took a nick name to himself from the fall and death of Alaafin's brother.

On page 192, paragraph 2 and page 193, section 3, of the History of the Yorubas, this same story is confirmed thus – "The watch word was now given 'O ya' *i.e.* Now is the time; and the whole army turned their swords upon the royal party and massacred them. Chief Opele of Gbogun was famous on that occasion, and took to himself a name 'A ri agada pa aburo Oba', *i.e.* (One who has a blade for slaying the king's brother").

"THE REBELLION OF THE OYO CHIEFS, *(note here, not of the whole country now called Yoruba country)*, was the heading of the following – "The death of the late King was all that the rebel chiefs demanded, after which the army entered the city, pillaged the palace, and dispersed, each to his own place. From this time, the spirit of rebellion and independence began to spread throughout the kingdom. Adebo was placed on the throne with the nominal title of King; but without the authority and power of a King. It was his misfortune to have come to the throne at such a time, and he held the scepter for only 130 days.

"Afonja the Kakanfo of Ilorin and Opele, the Baale of Gbogun were the first to proclaim their independence; other chiefs soon followed their example. This was the commencement of the breakup of the unity of the Yoruba Kingdom and the beginning of the tribal independence. Tribute was no longer paid to the King. The King's messengers and Ilaris no longer carried that dread as before, nor were they allowed to oppress people or enrich themselves with their goods as before."

ORIGINAL FOUNDER AND SETTLERS OF IBADAN

Although the former Ibadan, situated somewhere near the site of the present one was, twice founded by an Ife man, named Lade-edu whom other people call Lagelu, yet, the present Ibadan, which was formerly a farm of the Egbas of Erunmu and the other neighbouring towns, was first made a real living town by the combined army of the Ifes and Ijebus, who conquered the town of Owu, round about 1816 A.D.

Ephemeral Reduction of Alaafin's Power

Though Opele and Afonja, with their followers rebelled against and refused to serve the Alaafin any longer, yet there were others who would not like to see Alaafin to be so perpetually degraded. Therefore, there not arose series of civil wars in the Yoruba country to the extent that those who were not willing to serve Alaafin resolved to leave his territory entirely. That was why they came in great numbers to settle in Ifes towns of Ibadan, Ikire, Aponmu, Gbongan, Ikoyi, etc.

Seeing after some years that those people were cordially received by the Ifes, the other Oyos, attacked by the Fulani, came to join them in the Ife districts.

To confirm this, vide The History of the Yorubas, page 228, paragraph 1, reading thus –

(a) "The metropolis had long been left to herself whilst great and stirring events had been taking place all over the country. The outcome of the rebellion of the Chiefs and the revolution was the foundation of modern Ibadan, Abeokuta, Modakeke, the occupation of Ijaye, Abemo, the destruction of Owu, and the fall of many ancient towns in the plain, and above all, the ascendancy of Ilorin under the ravaging foreigners."

(b) Page 230, paragraph 1, reads thus – "By the Fulani conquest of all the principal towns in Yoruba proper, fugitives from all parts escaped southwards and settled in all Ife towns except at Ile-Ife, the chief town. They were in great numbers at Moro, Ipetumodu, Odunabon, Yakioyo, Ifa-lende, Sope, Waro, Ogi as well as Aponmu and Ikire."

RECEPTIONS OF THE OYOS AT IBADAN

When the Oyos first came, the Ifes housed and treated them so kindly that both lived together in all Ife towns without any distinction. Evidence was borne to this point by an aged Modakeke man when Sir Alfred C. Moloney, the first Governor of Lagos was making enquiry into the causes of the trouble between the Ibadans and Modakekes on one side, and the Ifes on the other side, as contained in the History of the Yorubas, page 525, and paragraph 2, thus: "An old man, of probably about 100 years of age was sent for, and he came, leaning upon a staff, he was a boy when Modakeke was settled. The main object in giving the history of Modakeke was to rebut the oft repeated that they were slaves to the Ifes. He stated *(as we have learnt above)* that they were originally refugees from the ancient Oyo Provinces, who escaped south when the Fulanis became masters of the country. They were well received at first at Ife, and treated with much sympathy and cordiality, but the turning point of the cordial relation came when Maye, the Ife general was expelled from Ibadan, and the Oyos gained ascendency in that town.

As a sign of long, goodwill of the Ifes towards the Oyos of their towns, the Modakekes lived with the Ifes in the same town without any distinction during the reigns of the following Oonis – (1) Odunle; (2) Gbanlare; (3) Gbegbaje; (4)and Wunmonje, before Adegunle Abewela, the Ooni who gave Modakeke to the Oyos was born; because his mother was married by an Ife prince from among the Oyos, many years after the Oyos had come to settle among the Ifes.

To start with, readers are wished to know that during the time under discussion, neither the Oyos, nor any other people of our race were known as Yorubas; and hence, the application of "Oyos" to all the people from and in the Alaafin's Kingdom.

More proof of this was given by Chief I.B. Akinyele, the Olubadan of Ibadan in his first history of Ibadan, page 27, paragraph 6, reading thus – "Lakoko yi, awon Ife ni won poju ti won si l'agbara ju, awon ni won si je ogagun, awon ni awon Oyo ati Ijebu si fi okan te, awon ni won si je pataki awon ti nwon te Ibadan do lakoko yi." (At this time, the Ifes were the most numerous, most powerful, and they were the head of all the war chiefs; and it was upon them that both Oyos and the Ijebus depended. Finally, they were of all the settlers of Ibadan at this time, the most important.)

THE MODERN YORUBA COUNTRY AND ITS EXTENT

It is to be recollected that it has been previously told that it was the early C.M.S. missionaries to our country that gave us all the name Yorubas about 1856 A.D. It is very gratifying to note that, not only did they give us this name, but they did not fail to give us the graphic extent of their new Yoruba country as contained on page 69, of a book containing various papers read by the specialists on each of the subjects dealt with in the Conference of the C.M.S. Clergymen, held at Ibadan from 23rd to 26th January, 1899, where and when Bishop C. Phillips, late of Ondo, stated thus – "From the above remarks, it is evident that the tribes comprising this large nation, to which we apply the name Yoruba may be enumerated as follows –

The Egbados	Barapas	Yorubas	Egbas
Ijebus	Ifes	Ondos	Ijeshas
Ekitis	Igbominas	Bunus	Benin, *with its dependencies*
Sekiris	Ijos	Atico	Idowanis and Owos.

It will now be clearly seen that not only was the whole of the ancient Yoruba country absorbed in the modern one, but Alaafin ceased to be head, giving place to Ooni, who was, and still is, the real overlord of the whole new kingdom.

The fact that Alaafin was the head of the first Yoruba country which is now included in the newer and more extensive Yoruba country has made many people believe that Alaafin is still the overlord of our whole country, and that Ooni is his mere high priest, in a more refined form "The Spiritual Head of the whole Yoruba country."

As the true relative position of the Ooni to those of the other Obas will be dealt with separately in another history, the importance of Ooni will be briefly shown here.

THE BASES OF THE NEW YORUBA COUNTRY

It may be asked why the missionaries, who gave us all the name Yorubas, in the nineteenth century, were able to bring all the towns grievously mentioned into the catalogue of their formed Yoruba country.

The simple answer to such a question is not more than that their reason for doing so was based on these two factors – (1) test of language, and (2) test of a common origin.

On these two points, Bishop C. Phillips stated in the Ibadan Conference of the Clergymen of 23rd-26th January, 1899 thus – "If we apply the test of language, we will find that the national language is the same, although the dialectic differences are so great that a member of one tribe often requires an interpreter in the first instance before he can converse with his brother of another tribe. But a few weeks' intercourse, both parties will soon find that, in spite of the differences in the formation of words, and in the names of various objects, their language is radically identical.

119

"By the test of language, I think we can claim the Bunu tribe, whose territory extends to the banks of the Niger, near Lokoja and the Igbiras, who migrated to the opposite bank of that river, and the Igbominas, who occupy the north-eastern corner beyond the Ekiti country, as belonging to this nation, as well as the Jekiris or Sekiris, who inhabit the isles near the Ocean, which are formed by the estuaries of the Benin river, whose language is only a gross corruption of a common origin from Ile-Ife.

"If we also apply the test of a common origin, we can still claim many more people as belonging to this large nation. Dispersed as the tribes are, over a large extent of country, alienated and disaffected to each other as they are, by intertribal wars, and cut off as they are, from all mutual intercourse by ages of estrangement, yet we find that each of them preserves the tradition of their common origin from Ile-Ife, which they still esteem as the Eden of the nation, from whence they migrated to the different territories which they now occupy. And I think we are right in claiming all the people among whom this tradition is found as members of the Yoruba nation. By this test we can reckon the Benin people as one of our tribes, although their language is unintelligible to us. Until this day, none of our different tribes would omit to name the Benin King in the same family list with the Alaafin of Oyo, the Alake of Abeokuta, the Awujale of Ijebu, Alakehi of Ketu, the Ooni of Ife, and the Benin King himself acknowledged this relationship. In 1887, just after the Lagos Government had established an armistice between the belligerents, he sent an embassy, consisting of about 50 persons, whose avowed object was to repair the breach made in his father's house at Ile-Ife. The embassy went through the Ondo country, and stayed a few months in the Ife camp, and returned by the same way to Benin.

"If the Benin people form a part of the Yoruba nation, it follows that all other tribes which owe allegiance to the Benin King must also belong to the nation."

Some writers have made the reading public to know that, (1) At a certain time, the Yoruba capital was removed by Oranmiyan to Oyo or Oko, leaving a mere slave called Adimula to take care of the treasury and to worship the national deities for the Alaafin.

If this were correct, why did the Benin King not to Oyo, a place to which his father's capital had been removed? On the other land, why did Alaafin not query the Ooni of Ife for receiving the honour which was not due to him? Again, if as some people take it to mean today that the Oba of Benin was the eldest son of Oodua, and that Ooni was a mere slave, why did the former regard the latter as his father, whose house he sent 50 men to repair in 1887 A.D.?

This point will be better dealt with later on.

REAL POSITION OF OONI

According to the representation which some missionaries made to the Lagos Government, Alaafin began to be recognized as the overlord of our whole country as from 1886, and not earlier. In 1888, the Government signed an agreement with him as the overlord of all our land, and as the one to whom they could come for anything wanted in the whole of our Yorubaland. As luck would have it, a test case came to prove the authenticity of Ooni's real position amongst the Obas of our country.

It happened that during the term of office of His Excellency, Sir William MacGregor, a sharp dispute broke out between the Akarigbo and Elepe of Ijebu-Remo over the grave question of whether only one of these two Natural Rulers, or both have equal right to wear a crown each.

The argument on either side were so strong and heated that the matter was eventually brought to the notice of the Governor. As such a delicate matter could not be easily and properly handled without the assistance of the head of the race, the Governor quickly asked the Alaafin of Oyo to help him out of the serious situation. In order, therefore, to maintain the usurpatory position, Alaafin sent his messengers to the two contending parties, who rigorously queried his authority for coming between them in such an important matter which was beyond his power, position and knowledge. His messengers were disgracefully sent back to him.

Being not pleased with the disquieting situation, the Governor asked the two fighting rulers whether there was any other higher authority than the Alaafin in the whole of our country. They answered in the affirmative, and the Governor asked for who it was, and they told him that the Ooni of Ife alone was the only one who could decide such a case in the whole of this country. It was a great surprise to the Governor to hear such an astounding story; nevertheless, he set out to find out from other sources whether what he heard from those two fighting rulers was everywhere corroborated. The Governor was, therefore, obliged to invite the then Ooni Adelekan, commonly known as Olubuse to Lagos in the month of February, 1903.

At first, Ooni declined the invitation to Lagos on the grounds that no other Oba of our land had any right of seeing his face, and that if he was out of his town for some days together, something dreadful would happen in the whole country. The Governor asked whether anything could be done to avert any mishap which was likely to follow his leaving his town for Lagos; and Ooni replied that there was; but he hadn't enough money to run its expenses. The Governor said that he should not worry about the cost of it if only he was ready to honour his invitation. Then the Ooni agreed to come to Lagos at the above stated time. Nevertheless, the destruction of corn and banana fields of 1903, and 1904 by certain insects called "Tapi i", and the clouds of locusts was almost everywhere ascribed to Ooni's going to Lagos.

OONI'S EVIDENCE

On reaching Lagos, the Governor told the Ooni his main object of inviting him to Lagos. Having listened very carefully, to the statements of the two contending parties and the Governor's speech, the Ooni openly and definitely said that the two quarrelling Obas were his children, and that both were entitled to wear a crown each. After he had given the history of how and when each of them left Ile-Ife, the two Obas, disputing, as well as the Governor were entirely satisfied.

Being extremely pleased with the way and manner in which the Ooni creditably discharged his selfless Official and paternal duty, His Excellency Sir W. MacGregor promised to come and see him in his capital town.

According to his faithful promise, His Excellency the Governor visited Ile-Ife that year. When he reached there, he was astonished to find the Ooni of Ife, the accredited head of the whole Yoruba race in a very pitiable condition of having neither a good dwelling house, nor a single village as his territory, although he was not the originator of the long war between the Ibadans and the Ekitiparapos. When the Governor asked for what was responsible for Ooni's poor condition, the latter showed to the former, a copy of the treaty signed and ratify by all the powers of our country on Thursday, 23rd, September, 1886, at Kiriji, but which remained unfulfilled by the Ibadans and Modakekes. The Governor was so sorry that he promised to see to it that

Ooni's territory was returned to him as far as the Osun River, in perfect accordance with the term of the Treaty of 1886, and that immediately.

Although till this day, the boundary between Ife and Ibadan has not been properly fixed in agreement with that Treaty, yet, before Governor MacGregor went away entirely from Nigeria in 1904, he did his best before Ife boundary between Ibadan could be removed from where the Ife Post Office is today to Shasha River, instead of Osun River, in the Treaty. Limitation of time did not allow him to bring it to Osun before he left.

As a result of Sir W. MacGregor's observation and candid opinion of the Ooni's position, read below, what was written in Gazette No.9, page 170 of 1903, reading as follows — "The Governor then observed that it reflected very great discredit on the Yoruba people to have allowed the Ooni of Ife, the acknowledged Head of the most distinguished and honourable family of all Yorubas to live in a roofless house. His Excellency suggested that it would be of a good thing if all other great Chiefs rendered the Ooni some assistance and build his house for him. His Excellency promised to do all he could to help the Ooni."

This same incident was attested to by Dr. O. Johnson at page 647, and a portion of paragraph 2 of the History of the Yorubas thus — Sir William MacGregor, during his regime as Governor, among other places, visited Ile-Ife. He granted the Owoni an animal subsidy on account of his position."

Here comes a query to be answered by those who continue to believe that Alaafin is the head of our whole country, and that Ooni is only a high priest, who was once the son of a sacrificial slave.

Similarly, when MacGregor saw clearly that the Government had been misled by a few missionaries in recognizing Alaafin as the true head of the whole Yoruba country, instead of Ooni of Ife, he gave Ooni his full right.

WHY OONI WAS RECOGNISED BY THE GOVERNMENT

Besides all that has been said, there may be some people who will still condemn Governor MacGregor's act of recognizing Ooni as the real head of our whole race. For the information of such people, references will be briefly made here to the main purpose of the British Government, in sending Captain (afterwards) Lord F.D. Lugard, the first Governor-General of Nigeria to Nigeria for the first time.

When the Royal Niger Company was administering the Government of the Protectorates of Nigeria, among the places under its jurisdiction were Ilorin, Nupe land, Borgu and Bussa. In order that they might be able to run their government effectively well, and at the same time, carry on their trade smoothly, they first signed treaties with the acknowledged overlord of each, or group of towns in the area under their influence. Borgu, a town near Ilorin, was one of the outstanding cases of the time.

At first, when the Company learnt that the Chief of Bussa was the overlord of the Chief of Borgu, they signed a treaty with him on behalf of the Chief of Borgu and himself. In 1893, the French Government, on the strength of the privilege which the Berlin Conference of 1885 gave them, declared a Protectorate over Dahomey. A year later, they came to know that the Chief of Nikki, in the hollow bend between the North-Western side of Nigeria and the North-Eastern side of Dahomey, was the overlord of Bussa, which had long been in the territory of the Niger Company.

To be able to get all these places, the French Government sent Captain Decouer with 500 Senegalese on the 24th of July, 1894, to go and conclude a treaty with the Chief of Nikki, so that Bussa and Borgu, which were already in the territory of the Niger Company might be in their possession.

Learning what the French had done, the British Government dispatched Captain (afterwards) Lord Lugard with 24 men on the 28 of the same month, with the definite instructions of outrunning Captain Decouer, and of signing a treaty with the Chief there before the arrival of Decouer.

Accordingly, Lugard outran Decouer and signed a treaty with the Chief of Nikki on behalf of both Bussa and Borgu; and that is why both places are in the British Nigeria today.

Five days after Lugard's arrival at Nikki, the treaty was ratified and he returned to begin his administrative work in Nigeria. On his return journey, he and the French ambassador–Decouer, came across each other on the Niger.

The disappointment which the French met, in this matter, nearly caused a very serious war between them and the British. Nevertheless, when the British Government had given honour to whom the honour of being the overlord of those places was due, everything was eventually amicably settled.

His Highness The Ooni Adelekan

Commonly know as Olubuse, reigned from 1893 - 1910. He was the one who, at the invitation of His Excellency, Sir William Macgregor, settled the Crown dispute between Akarigbo and Elepe, both of Sagamu in February, 1903. Then the Governor agreed that Ooni was the father of all Obas

NOT CIRCUMSTANTIAL

Some people may think that the matter which led Sir MacGregor to the conclusion of recognizing Ooni's genuine headship over the whole Yoruba country might be a mere circumstantial one. In order to show that the Governor's act was properly based on the precious behaviours of all the powers of our land towards the Ooni before some missionaries stole themselves in so as to be able to confuse the anciently smooth running order of things, in order that they might be able to push Alaafin forward as head of our whole land, the following points are brought out for the readers.

Although The History of the Yoruba was written by a few of such missionaries, yet it is thought that no better authority than a portion of their work can be cited. Therefore; the attention of the readers is drawn to the under quoted passages —

The History of the Yorubas, page 467, reads in part as follows: "The fact was that Derin (then Ooni elect of Ife) was elated by the honour and respect accorded him by all the powers, and also by the recognition of the Governor. He thought it was because he was an Ife, a city which tradition says was the cradle of mankind, and not because he happened to hold the key of the situation to lock against or open for the Ibadans to obtain ammunition from the Coast."

In order that readers may be able to know why the Ooni elect, openly and boldly made the above referred to assertion, another passage will be quoted to show what a few of those missionaries said about him.

The History of the Yorubas, page 458, paragraph 5, reads thus – "Derin the Chief of Oke-Igbo, now the Owoni elect of Ife, seemed at this time to have the key of the whole situation in his hands and his favour and goodwill were sought by all. The Ibadans sent him slaves and excellent native cloths and other valuables as presents that he might keep the road open. The Ilorin sent him horses, the Ekiti Kings sent him baskets of kola nuts, and other valuable presents came also from Ijebu and from Abeokuta that he might keep the road closed."

It is evidently certain that, all the various tribes mentioned above did not use the same road, and however expert the Ooni elect might be in road keeping, he could not keep Egba, Ijebu, Ibadan, Ilorin and Ekiti roads open or close for them at the same time. If, on the other hand, Ooni had to keep the roads open, or close, it means, he had to be the arch enemy of the powers of our land, because from time to time, he had to be fighting for one against the other. Therefore, the fact that they all honoured and respected him in addition to the various valuable things frequently sent to him as presents showed that all the powers of our country recognized and accepted the suzerainty of the Ooni as their real head then.

How Ooni Could Enjoy Governor's Recognition Then

It may be asked how, in those long gone by days Ooni, who was very far away from the Coast could enjoy Governor's recognition, when no other Oba of our land had similar privilege.

The simple reason for this was, although Lagos alone was at that time directly under the British rule, yet, it was a common habit of the Officers of the British Government to visit all friendly neighbouring towns to Lagos.

In order to clarify this point, it is deemed necessary to refer to a part of the letter, written at Government House, Lagos, on 14th April, 1882, by Sir Samuel Rowe, the

Governor-General of Gold Coast, under whom the supervision of Lagos then was.

On the 15th of October, 1881, some missionaries wrote two letters to Lagos, one to Lieutenant Governor W.B. Griffiths, and the other to the Rev. J.B. Wood, one of the C.M.S. Missionaries, who would help them to influence the Governor to recognize Alaafin as the titular head of the whole Yoruba race. To be able to achieve their aim in view they brought the question of the settlement of the Kiriji war before the Governor.

As a consequence, the Governor of Lagos reported the matter to the Governor-General, whose reply goes thus – "I have carefully thought over the message you gave to me a fortnight ago, and I have heard from the Lieutenant Governor all what passed in the matter before I came to Lagos.

"I appreciate the action of the King of Oyo in sending to the Governor of Lagos to ask him to send an officer to make peace between the Ibadans and Ijebus. I thank the King of Oyo for the compliment he has paid to the English Government in doing this, showing that he believes in the honour of the English Government and that he feels confident that an Officer from the English Government will deal justly in this matter.

"The great Queen whom I serve, Her Gracious Majesty, the Queen of England and Empress of India, has no other wishes than good wishes towards the entire African people. Her Majesty's instructions to her officers whom she sent to govern this colony are to promote by all proper means, friendly intercourse between the people under their rule and the native tribes living near them.

"In doing this from time to time, Her Majesty has approved the visits of Her officers to many of the tribes neighbouring Lagos. But Her Majesty has no desire to bring the inland tribes neighbouring Lagos under British rule, and though wicked people have said that if white man comes to the interior he will take the country, I tell you publicly that my Queen has no wish to take your country."

Before the officers could visit a country then, they used to ask for the head of the whole place. Therefore, Ooni being the first person recommended to them as the accredited head of our country, the Governor recognized him as such as related above.

Why Ooni is Known As True Head of The New Yoruba Country

It is certainly sure that many people will like to know why and when Ooni of Ife became the supreme head of the newly formed Yoruba Kingdom.

The answer to this all important question, may be divided into two *viz*, (1) ancient, and (2) modern.

(a) In regard to the ancient greatness of the Ooni, readers are directed to page 90 of Iwe Kika Ekarun Li Ede Yoruba, paragraphs 1-3, reading as follows – "Historians said that, very many years ago, there was at Ile-Ife a man, whose name was Lagelu, Oro-Apata-Maja. A real great man was he at Ile-Ife. He had a well recognized chieftaincy, and was very brave. His chieftaincy was so important that it could be unhesitatingly called the Balogun title of the present day."

"One fine morning, Lagelu was suddenly seen getting ready with his children, wives and several of his relatives to leave the town, saying that he was going to carve a town of his own. This kind of attempt was then not a new one, and it was never once related that such a practice did any time evoke Ooni, the King of Ile-Ife's *(not a slave)* annoyance. His attitude gave immeasurable advantage to many valiants, who likewise left the town to found other towns in several other places, and became Bales *(not actual kings then)* of their towns; nevertheless, they never failed to acknowledge the suzerainty of the Ooni as their King *(not as a High priest then)*. Without much ado, this is what brought about that saying, "Ile-Ife is the cradle of the whole Yoruba race, as well as that of the whole universe."

"The town which Lagelu carved after leaving Ile-Ife as previously stated is called Ibadan today."

The thorough knowledge of this fact, aided Bishop C. Phillips late of Ondo, and the illustrations father of His Lordship, Bishop S.C. Phillips, the Vicar – General of Osogbo, in the Conference of the Clergymen, held from 23-26 January, 1899 at Ibadan, to make the following statements among others – "Dispersed as the tribes are, over a large extent of country, alienated and disaffected to each other as they are, by intertribal wars, and cut off as they are, from all mutual intercourse by ages of estrangement yet, we find that each of them preserved the tradition of their common origin from Ile-Ife, which they still esteem as the Eden of the nation from whence they migrated to the different territories which they now occupy. And I think we are right in claiming all the people among whom this tradition is found as members of the Yoruba nation."

Winding up this part of the History, it will be recalled that during the span of time they all were together at Ile-Ife they had no other name than "Ifes". Therefore, so long as they still preserve the tradition of their common origin from Ile-Ife, it is still more essential to preserve the tradition of the original common name than to bear a forced name "YORUBA."

IFE, CRADLE OF THE YORUBA PART II

THE IFE TOWN

Of all the dependent countries of the British Commonwealth of Nations today, Nigeria, with her teeming various resources is, by far, the largest, and yet, until recently, she was very much unknown not only to the Europeans in general, but also to many important English people under whose direct rule she is.

As it was with Nigeria in general, so also it is with Ile-Ife in particular; because even till now, many people do not know the exact situation of Ile-Ife, either on the map of Nigeria or otherwise nor do they know why it is regarded and called the "cradle" not only of the Yoruba race, but also of the whole universe. Above all, how Ile-Ife came into existence is, till this day a stupendous problem to the world at large. Consequently, many people started to say that Yorubas must have come from either Egypt or Mecca, with any of which we have no blood relationship at all.

POSITION

Ile-Ife is situated at a place about 54 miles north-east of Ibadan 20 miles south of Ilesa, and 31 miles north-west of Ondo.

It is a well watered area, and is very rich in many agricultural products, big and small birds. The only reasonable, and to a certain extent, dependable forest reserve it has today lies between Ondo and Ijebu forest reserves, all of which are said to be yet bound in elephants and other big animals.

In ancient times, Ile-Ife was the chief place where the then known most valuable ornamental beads called "Segi and Erinla" were mostly dug up from their several feet deep beds of earthen hidden places.

From time immemorial, until 1907, all the chief roads leading from the coastal towns through Abeokuta and Ijebu on the one hand, and those leading from other places like Oyo, Iseyin, etc., on the other hand, seemed to commerge at Ibadan, from where they formed only one main road through Ile-Ife to Ekiti country, Owo, and Benin City respectively. In addition, the Ijebus and the Ondos, who are the immediate neighbours of the Ifes on the south had two other separate routes, which also commerged at Ita-Ijamo, on the Isoya road of Ife. The change that came to make Ile-Ife almost a lonesome corner afterwards happened when the Nigerian Railway reached the town of Osogbo in the year 1907.

In order that the people living near the railway lines might have outlets to the rail lines, small and major roads were started to be made before that year. One of such major roads then built was that of Osogbo to Ilesa. Therefore, by means of the railway carrying coastal people to Osogbo, and major roads leading people from Osogbo to Ilesa and up countries, the people using that road soon found that the Osogbo to Ilesa road would serve their desired purposes much better than that of Ile-Ife, which they had long been using. Therefore, when the Ife to Ilesa roads was constructed, it became only one of the feeding roads to that of Ilesa to up countries. That was why both Ile-Ife and Iperindo are no longer spoken of as important places today as they were before.

Some people sometimes think that the present Ile-Ife was not the same as the one in which Oodua lived and reigned; but readers are here definitely told that there has never been a second Ile-Ife anywhere in the world since the world began, and if perchance there happens to be another one elsewhere, the one which is known to many people today was the same in which Oodua lived, reigned and died as the first Ooni of Ife. The route by which he entered the town, and the offsprings of the Chief who escorted him to the town are still in the same town today. The memory of Oodua's royal entry is always commemorated on the Coronation Day of every new Ooni at the very spot where Oodua was first met by their great great grandfather.

In honour of his first entry into the town by way of Mo-ore Gate, on the way to Ilesa, all the important national things to be done in the town must be made to start from that historical gate till today. Consequently, although each quarter of Ile-Ife has its own state head-guard, named "Lodoko", yet that of Mo-ore is the head of the mall till even date.

AREA AND POPULATION

The area of the whole Nigeria is roughly estimated at 373,000 square miles, and its population is similarly said to be somewhat like 32 million. Out of these, the area of our today known Yoruba country is considered to be 46,900 square miles, and its population is approximately 5,000,000. Further still, for the purpose of close relationship, it is hoped that it will be very interesting to the readers to know that, in almost every other thing, except in dialect, which afterwards evolved into a separate language of their own, the Benin people are part and parcel of the present day Yoruba race. If therefore, the area of land of 8,600 square miles occupied by them, and their roughly calculated population of over 483,000 be respectively added to those already assigned to the Yorubas, the augmented area and population of the Ife country will suddenly become astoundingly larger and higher than they previously were.

On the other hand, if the accounts of some Ibo historians be envisaged and absolutely accepted as being authentic that, up to date, majority of the Ibo people can with certainty trace their origin from Ile-Ife, then it will, for the purpose of history, be necessary to include their population *(especially that of Arochuku)* into the Ife area of influence.

The Ibos are briefly referred to here because there are not all altogether lacking today some living and accredited Ibo historians, especially those of Arochuku, who can boldly and unhesitatingly trace the history of their origin back to Ile-Ife.

Such briefly, is, the position of Ife.

IFE, THE CRADLE OF THE UNIVERSE, NOT ONLY OF THE YORUBAS

So long as it has been proved to some reasonable extent that not a single one of the places already mentioned as being the original home of the Yorubas is capable of being given such a high honour, the spontaneous question that is likely to come from every conscientious readers is, "Where then is the origin of the Yorubas?"

That Ile-Ife is the cradle of the Yorubas is a well known and universally accepted fact; but it opens to a doubt as to whether anyone has ever tried to find out what precisely is meant by the word "cradle".

According to English Dictionary, the word "cradle" means, a bed or crib in which children are rocked; the place where one is born and brought up; infancy; a frame in which anything is imbedded.

Naturally, any impartial reader will know that what was in the mind of the first people who gave Ile-Ife the name of the "cradle of the Yoruba race" was nothing short of the idea that Ile-Ife is the place where Yorubas were born and bred. This name was not simply given to Ile-Ife by the Ifes themselves, but it was first given to her by the outsiders, who knew the real and true position of Ile-Ife in relation to those of the other towns of our country.

Nearly all, if not all English speaking people know the meaning of the word – cradle. If therefore, it has been used wrongly in connection with Ile-Ife it therefore ought to have been corrected and changed.

It cannot but be said that, it is a great insult to the Ifes to tell them that they came originally from either Mecca or Upper Egypt; and worse still, that they came from either Nubia or Hausaland to settle at Ile-Ife. If there are some of them who agree that the Ifes came from any of the above mentioned places, it means either they simply want to please the public against their conscience, or they are ignorant of the real facts. It is very significant to see that the idea of the Ifes is exactly the same as the notion contained in the phrase "Ile-Ife, the cradle of the Yoruba race". Perhaps the underwritten statements will help us to understand the whole situation much better.

Although Ile-Ife is not mentioned in the Bible History, yet the analogy which her received history bears to the Bible History in some parts makes it feasible for us to touch briefly on Ife History here. At Ile-Ife, the names of some important persons and places are so almost identical with the names of some of the Biblical characters and places that one is inclined to think that there was a certain amount of close similarity between the ancient Ifes and some of the people of the Old Testament time. Here are a few of such names:

(1) Oodua, now pronounced and written "ODUDUWA" was described to be similar, not only in name but also in work to "Noah"

(2) The reported work of Olu-oro-gbo, otherwise called "Omoluorogbo", by some people was said to be much more

like that of Moses, the emancipator of the Hebrews than that of Jesus Christ, the Saviour of Mankind, Olu-oro-gbo was reported to go up to heaven thrice a day to plead with God for the Ifes in the same way as Moses went up in the mountains twice to plead with God for the Israelites for forty consecutive days on each occasion. His frequent going to heaven on behalf of the Ifes made the people give him the name of "Messenger between God and Man" , that is, Iko-Ajalaye, Iko-Ajalorun".

(3) The name of Moremi, a woman deliverer of the Ifes from their cunning and wicked kinsmen, called "Igbos", is almost like that of Aaron's elder sister Miriam, who led an army of women in singing praises unto the Lord after the triumphal crossing of the Red Sea by the Israelites on their journey from Egypt to Cannon. In this respect, MARY, the mother of Jesus cannot be compared with Moremi, in that the former did not at any time take part in any public heroic demonstration as did the latter. On the other hand, Christianity did not come to Ile-Ife through Olu-oro-gbo as many people think. It is by regarding Olu-oro-gbo as Jesus Christ, that many people suggest that Moremi, as his mother must be regarded as Mary, the mother of the Saviour of the whole world. Moses was the deliverer of only the Jews from Egypt and from God's wrath; but was never the Saviour of Mankind as Jesus was.

In the second place, it is nowhere related that Jesus did at any time hold a stone as tablet as Moses did whenever he went up to pray, nor had He a Pepple – Stool as Olu-oro-gbo had.

Olu-oro-gbo was more like Moses than he was like Jesus in that his Pepple-stool was after his death worshipped at a place called "Lafogido" as god of stool (i.e.) "Orisa Apoti" in the same way as the Brazen Serpent of Moses was worshipped by the Israelites, who named it Nehushtan after his death.

(4) The name of Oke-Ora, that is, Oramife's Hill, is similar to Mount Ararat of the Bible History.

As for Oramife, it was, and still is, strongly believed by all non Christians and Muslims of Ife that, of all the many heroes worshipped at Ile-Ife, Oramife alone was not once a human being, while the other were human beings originally; and hence no human sacrifice has ever been offered to him. It is said that Oramife has his palace built of fire in heaven, and his earthly house built on Ora-Hill at a place between Ile-Ife and Itagunmodi in Ilesa territory.

For the two terms, "Fiery house and House on Hill" respectively, Oramife was given the nick names of "Onile-Ina and Onile-Ori-Oke" respectively.

The name Oramife means, the maker or moulder of the Ifes. In ancient time, Oramife was regarded as the God of Heaven and earth; and he, on the other hand was answering them accordingly. The Ifes' worship of Oramife was almost identical with the Jewish way of worshipping Jehovah God.

The worship of Oramife was, and still is, in the hands of Chiefs Obaluru and Oluroye of Mo-ore quarter. Oramife been regarded as the most superior of all the worshipped heroes, the Ifes envisaged him to be the controller of not only the air, but also of every other element.

In the days of old, there were many successive well recognized Oramife's prophets, called and known by the name of "Ay'orunbo" which implies, People who paid regular visits to heaven and returned". The main duty of such prophets was the revelation of the things seen in their dreams or visions to the people of the town as a whole, and equally so to individuals. In short, they were carrier of Oramife's messages to the Ifes of old.

Their method of receiving messages was quite unique and strange. Each Ay'orunbo, or Prophet was reported to have to sleep for from three to five days together before he woke up. The duration of sleep depended upon the nature of the messages with which an Ay'orunbo was entrusted. It was on account of their unusual long sleeps that they were given the name of Ay'orunbo.

This kind of age long practice was continuously in vogue at Ile-Ife till round about the year 1913 or 1914, when the last of them named, Aje died. The writer of this history knew this Aje as well as his immediate predecessor in office, named Fagbola of Obele's house at Ojafe in Mo-ore quarter personally.

Of all the Ay'orunbo of Ife, Awodina was by far the most famous and respected. He was to the Ifes, what Prophet Isaiah was to the Jews. The next renowned Ay'orunbo after him was Aroje, who was still alive about the year 1891 or 1892. These two had definitely told the Ifes very many years ago, the various types of things now experienced in the world.

It is particularly worthy of notice that the practice of having Ay'orunbos, automatically ceased at Ile-Ife, only when Christianity was actually embraced by a large majority of the Ifes during the ministerial period of that energetic and faithful servant of Christ – the Rev Arthur Josephus Williams, of the blessed memory, whom the Ifes shall never forget. May he rest in peace.

According to the Ife Received History, Oramife was said to be the owner of the whole world, and that the Ifes were his chosen people, in the same way as the Israelites were, of Jehovah God in ancient time. For this reason, the Ifes usually sing as follows during "Agbon Festival" thus –

(1) Ora lomo n'Ife, Eelu gbogbo Ora lo n'Ife (2) Ora lomo ni'le, Eelu gbogbo Ora lo ni'le. *Tune* – d : d : m : d : r . d : m : r : m : d : s : s : t : l : s :

The first of these two lines means, Oramife is the owner of Ife. The second signifies that Oramife is the owner of the whole earth. On account of these statements, the Ifes claim that not only the whole black race, but also the whole universe had its origin from Ile-Ife. Stories supporting this claim are not far fetched. One of such stories is the one which the Ife Received History tells us that, on account of a certain misunderstanding over some eggs, the white people, who chiefly fed on eggs then left Ile-Ife by way of Ijio, in Mo-ore. It is said that they went in the direction of Okun, or Ocean of Ile-Ife, now a very small pool at Ijio. The Osara, or Lagoon of Ile-Ife was not very far from this Okun. The site of Osara is very near the Christ Apostolic Church, Ile-Ife, on the way to Ilesa today.

Parts of the evidences supporting the Ife history are (1) The whites were the first people to use shoes and boots. (2) They also were the first people to show us the great value of the precious stone called Diamond. A tremendous importance was attached to this stone by the ancient Ifes, because the following two things were for hundreds of years prominently seen in the part of the city where it is related that the white people lived when they were at Ile-Ife: (a) Half a pair of stone, and (b) The Ijio Moon, which more enlightened people call a bold piece of Diamond today. Both these things were very near the Okun, or Ocean of Ijio. The Diamond had since about 1893 been found missing; but the half a pair of shoes was seen there up to the year 1922, and it is still believed to be in the city today. (Probably in the Ife Museum).

Another strong reason backing up the Ifes' claim is the statement made by Professor Leo Frobenius, the leader of the German expedition which visited Ile-Ife in 1910-1912 A.D. for the purpose of exploring the antiquities of Ife.

Professor Frobenius whom the writer as a schoolboy knew well, declared that he detected at Ile-Ife in his research work, a difference between the high class ancient

Yorubas, men of fine stature, extraordinary slenderness and delicacy of limbs, narrow heads, and fairer skins, and those of the lower classes who possess the usual negro characteristics.

On the strength of these things it is very much safe to assume that for some time, white and black men lived together at Ile-Ife as claimed by the Ife received history.

TRUTH GRADUALLY COMING OUT

The trouble with many people for not believing Ile-Ife as the cradle of Mankind may be divided into two sections thus – (a) The Garden of Eden, and (b) the Tower of Babel. It is a common belief of almost everybody in the world that, these two places are in Asia today; and consequently, everybody believes that Asia, and nowhere else in the world must have been the origin of Mankind; but in absolute point of facts, it may be definitely seen that those who believe that the cradle of Mankind is in Asia and not in Africa are very far from truth. Today, no one can point out the exact position of the Garden of anywhere, and therefore, it may not at all be correct to believe that it ever existed in the east at any time.

As a matter of fact, there was a very strong trace of similarity between the ancient Ifes and the builders of the Tower of Babel in that the Plain of Babel was not the original home of those who started to build a Tower there. It is definitely known that they came to that place from somewhere.

For the proof of this, *vide* the Book of Genesis, chapter XI, verses 1 and 2 (Revised Version) readings thus – "And it came to pass, as they journeyed east (towards) that they found a plain in the land of Shinar; and they dwelt there."

It is certainly sure that not only did they come from a

place to the Plain of Shinar, but they had become civilized before they reached there, and, therefore, like the ancient Ifes, they had already known how to build houses with strong materials like bricks.

For the proof of this, *vide* the Book of Genesis, chapter XI, verse 3, where it reads thus – "And they said one to another, Go to, let us make brick and burn them thoroughly. And they had brick for stone, and slime had they for morter."

This idea shows that the builders of the Tower of Babel had some resemblance to the ancient Ifes, who were known to be highly civilized from almost their very origin. Therefore, definite as it is, on the point that the Ifes did not come to Ile-Ife from any Asiatic country, so also it is, of the opinion of some writers that the builders of the Tower of Babel must have come out of Ile-Ife to that place; but perhaps not all at once.

If the story of a misunderstanding between the white people and the rest Ifes over some eggs were correct, it might mean that those white people, who left Ile-Ife, managed one way or another to go by way of Abyssinia which, of all African countries is, the only one on the same parallel line of Latitude with Nigeria, through which people could pass to either east Africa or Asia in those days. It is almost certain that other races equally took the same route and went as far as Abyssinia, and even beyond, until they came to settle in East Africa from where, after many years, some of them went over to Asia; probably at the time the continent of Africa was said to be one with the continent of Asia, and the Red Sea was regarded as an inland lake according to the finds of some geologists.

When the closeness of the two continents at the Gulf of Aden on the North-east of Africa, and at the old Isthmus of Suez (now Suez Canal) on the further north-east Africa is observed, one is inclined to take this suggestion as being correct.

Most likely, it was when they were on that march that they came to the Plain of Shinar where they started building the Tower of Babel.

EAST AFRICA IS SUGGESTED

It may be asked why it is suggested that East Africa might be the place to which the people who left Ile-Ife went after leaving the city. This is assumed because, up to a few years ago, the belief of about 99 percent of the people of the world was that, Asia was the origin of the world, and that we Africans, and especially the now Yorubas, came from that part of the world. But recently, we found that contrary to the belief of millions of people is the stubborn fact. This conclusion was arrived at in the writer's course of historical research work about 1945, and he was then prepared to voice out his opinion about it in hard words in due time; but to his greatest surprise, an unexpected support came to his view point in the wonderful discovery of Dr Leakey in East Africa.

In the issue of the Nigerian Daily Times of January 16, 1947, page 5, top part of columns 1 and 2, were printed the following striking points – "Where did man come from?" conference is to be held in Africa this month to try to answer that question.

"Fifty delegates from Britain, the U.S.A., France, Sweden, Italy, Belgium and other lands will attend, and I (Dr Kenneth Oakley), the Geologist go as the representative of the Natural History Museum.

"Dr L.S.B. Leakey, who found relics of the Stone Age in Kenya in 1942, has called the Conference. We shall examine and pass sentence on these finds (1) Fossilised apes, probably 30 million years old with human characteristics. (2) Pepple-tools and hand axes similar to ones found in Europe, but may be belonging to a much earlier period....possibly 125,000 years ago.

"These finds are preserved in lake deposits and caves of the East African Rift Valley and includes the famous site at Olorgesailie, near lake Magadi, which Dr Leakey has explored....Dr Leakey claims that these sites at Olorgesailie are the actual living sites of earliest man. They belong to what experts call the Acheulian stage of the "hand-axe culture."

If the discovery of Dr. Leakey refers to the people of the world before the Flood, then it confirms the argument that Asia was not, and cannot even be the original home of man in making as thousands of people have wrongly believed it; and, therefore for no earthly reason could the Yorubas have come from either Mecca or Egypt. If on the other hand, his discovery refers to the people of the world after the Flood, it can be said that the peoples of East Africa and Asia as well as others were a part of the various types of people who emigrated from Ile-Ife in search of more suitable dwelling places.

ANCIENT COMMON MISTAKES

When Genesis chapter xi, verse 1 of the Revised version was quoted to support the reason for believing Africa as the place from where the people who built the Tower of Babel came to settle in the Plain of Shinar, some well-read people might quote the Authorized Version of the same book and chapter and verse to contradict the previous statement.

Without careful reading, readers are likely to confuse the two issues which are really one and the same thing. The expression "As they journeyed from the east", as contained in the Authorized Version is, a mere wrong geographical expression, which was a common mistake of ancient people. For instance, Pitolemy, a Greek

145

Geographer of the second century, living at Alexandria, and who though was a more modern writer than the writers of the Bible time, yet made some outstanding mistakes.

Pitolemy was the first man to produce the map drawn on a frame work of the lines of Latitude and Longitude; and yet he underestimated the circumference of the globe, and showed on his map what in the Latin Version of his work is called "Terra Australia incognita" or the unknown Southland, whilst, he said the earth, and not the sun, was the centre of the Solar System.

Pitolemy's own conclusions were pure mistakes, all things considered; but the statement contained in the Authorized Version of the Bible was a mere wrong geographical expression which is not altogether a mistake at all.

Although we all know today that the earth is round like a ball, yet it took the people of the world several hundreds of years before this fact could really be accepted by scholars.

From the accepted idea that the earth is round like an orange, we know that if the earth is used and treated like a school wall map on being rolled in the direction of north to south, or West to east, we shall see that north and south will almost from the same thing and West and East will do likewise. It was the then lack of correct geographical knowledge of the four cardinal points of the earth that was responsible for "As they journey from east"; but when more correct knowledge of geography was acquired, more modern writers were able to put down what is read in the Revised Version thus – "As they journeyed east."

Now, to prove that not only the portion of the Scripture quoted from Revised Version, but also the opinions of some other eminent writers are the same as that of the writer, a portion of what Rev J.C. Hamer said under "The second peopling of the world", in his history book called "The

Old Testament History for young students" page 8, second paragraph will be quoted here thus – "The descendants of Japhet *(enlarged)* settled along the coasts of Mediterranean in Europe and Asia Minor, and spread northward and westward over Europe, and eastward as far as India. The race of Ham *(hot)* went southward, and settled principally in Africa, and the descendants of Shem *(renown)* made their abode for the most part in the south-west of Asia. But many of the early inhabitants still remained in the Plain of Shinar, and there, Nimrod, "the mighty hunter before the Lord", a grandson of Ham, founded a great empire with Babel or Babylon, for its capital, whence he extended his dominion northward, and found Nineveh and other cities. The descendants of Canaan, the youngest son of Ham, settled in Palestine which they called Canaan after their forefather.

Doubtlessly speaking, we, as well as those who claimed that our ancestors came from East, know that the Plain of Shinar, India, Japan, China and Palestine are all in the Far East.

If really Asia, and not Africa was the original home of man in making, from which of the above, or any other towns of Asia did the ancient people come to the other parts of the world where they live today, and what proofs has anybody to believe that the place is the true origin of mankind?

On the other hand, the facts that Ham was described as the progenitor of the black race, and that the important cities of Asia were founded by his offsprings, show clearly that it was the African people who went over to Asia to settle, and not Asiatic people that came to settle in Africa as people wrongly believe it to be.

Rev Mr Hamer says further that, after the descendants of Shem, Ham and Japhet had clean gone to their respective new homes, many of the original inhabitants of the Plain or Shinar were still left behind. If that was true of the people who journeyed to settle in the Plain of Shinar, it must be equally true that many of the inhabitants of the place from which they originally came to the Plain of Shinar; and, therefore, peopling of India should have been done by them rather than by the children of Japhet, because they were likely to be in greater number than the children of those who were a mere portion of them, because it is nowhere stated that the builders of the Tower of Babel left their original home with bag and baggage that no one remained there again.

It is furthermore read in Genesis chapter xi, verse 1, thus – "And the whole world was of one language and of one speech". Most likely, this was the condition of the world before, and not after the start of the building of the Tower of Babel. This shows clearly well that there were people in other parts of the world before the builders of the Tower came to the Plain of Shinar, because their movement towards east shows that they were coming from somewhere. Although Dr Leakey and his associates claim today, that East Africa was the site where man first lived, yet, it is most doubtful whether the world knew either Kenya or Olorgesailie to be in the east of any continent in the Old Testament time. Therefore, it cannot safely be claimed by anybody that any of these places can be the east referred to in the Bible stories.

THE COMING OF OODUA TO ILE-IFE

In talking of Egypt, a writer once gave the following axiomatic statement – "Nile is Egypt, and Egypt is Nile". This simply means, without Nile, there could be no Egypt; and equally so could there have been any importance attached to Nile without Egypt. In the same way can it be truly said that "Oodua is Ile-Ife, and Ile-Ife is Oodua", because whether we all are called either Ifes or Yorubas, no true history of our race will be consumated minus Oodua's name therein. Therefore, in order that the name of Oodua might be able to appear in all history books having reference to our race, every writer has made it an incumbent duty to popularize his book by leading the reading public to believe that Oodua might have come from one, or other of the places like Mecca, Nubia, Egypt or Sudan, to which references have been made in regard to the coming of the Yorubas. Nevertheless, it is here to be pointed out that the coming of Oodua to Ile-Ife was more mysterious than people think it to be. It is the mystery of it that led the people who wanted recognition for their writings to the idea that Lamirudu was Oodua's father and that Okanbi-Idekose-Iroaake was his first son, instead of Obalufon. In reality, Oodua was a man of no parentage.

It was and still is, yet believed by many historians that like some other important personalities, Oodua was not born, but curiously made before he came to Ile-Ife as a King.

That Oodua was no born, and consequently had no parentage, is well depicted in the story contained in a book entitled "Introducing West Africa", C.P.D. 1365/47 (H.R. 9N.4) page 78, and paragraphs 4-6 where it reads "Many Yoruba people in Southern Nigeria still believe that the City of Ife, about 120 miles, north-east of Lagos was the scene of the Creation. Accounts handed down by words of mouth say that originally, the earth was covered by water, but the Lord of heaven sent a priest, called Ojumu with a supply of magical sand. Ojumu threw the sand, and it was spread all over the earth by a five-fingered fowl, which the Lord of heaven had also sent to the earth. Dry land having appeared, the Lord of heaven charged Oodua to descend and establish a kingdom.

"Oodua descended by a chain, to the place where Ife

now stands, accompanied by sixteen elders; Orisa, one of the elders, then fashioned men and women.

"Archaeological discoveries at Ife show that a high developed civilization must have existed there. In 1938, for example, a number of bronze heads were discovered, which are outstanding works of art".

The above quoted statements and the finding and testimony are from independent body of people, who are by no means connected with Ile-Ife. The Ife Received History is only slightly different from what has just been stated above. Consequently, not only does the Ife History confirm the story that Ile-Ife is the cradle, not only of the Yoruba race, but of the whole universe. It also approves that at a certain period, Oramife, whom the Ifes regarded as the Lord of heaven or Controller of all the heavenly guns, destroyed all the living souls and things with a mighty deluge; and as a result, waters rested upon the surface of the earth for several months together. After many months, Oramife gave Oodua a handful magical sand and the five fingered fowl. He asked Oodua to throw both sand and the five fingered fowl down with orders that, as soon as they reached the water surface, the fowl should begin to spread the sand as far as it could.

After several months of doing this, the fowl came back to tell Oodua how far it had gone with the work. After praising the effort of the fowl, Oodua asked it to go back and spread it further in these words – "Lo tubo fe-e loju si i; lo tubo fe-e loju si i."

On other several occasion afterwards, the same fowl came to give the report of its work to Oodua; and on each subsequent occasion it received similar reply. This went on until the fowl did not return to him again.

Though the complete absence of the fowl served as an indication to Oodua that a large column of waters had been carried far away to where land and water meet today, yet, he was not actually certain of the extent of the solidarity of the ground upon which a reasonably large number of people could settle confidently, therefore, he sought Orunmila's advice on the vital matter in order that he and his people might not be carried away by water on landing where they had never been before.

In reply, Orunmila said that the appearing Odu governing Oodua's case was "Ejiogbe", whose citation runs thus: "Ologbon ogbon kole ta koko omi s'eti aso, Omoran-moran kole ka iye erupe ile, Alarinka kole de ibiti ile gbe pekun si, awon ni o da'fa fun Oodua nigbati yoo lo te ilu titun kan do". By a rough interpretation, it goes thus: "However clever a man may be, he cannot make a knot of water in the hem of his cloth. However witty a person may appear, he cannot make a correct computation of the number of the soil of the earth; and however extensively a person might have travelled in life, he can never reach the terminus of the land."

This indicated that Oodua could not of his own accord descend successfully without something being done. Therefore, Orunmila told him that before the landing could be favourable to him, Oodua had to offer a chain rope in sacrifice, because it was by that chain rope that they all must descend the Hill.

Before the ceremony was performed, Oodua informed all his principal followers. After they all had approved of the plan, Orunmila said that in order to alleviate Oodua's apprehension of the probable remaining water on the surface of the earth, he (Orunmila) would go down first by means of that chain rope according to the direction of his oracle, and that Obatala, their artist should follow him almost immediately to test the solidity of the soil. He said that if there was no space for them to stay, then they would climb up back by the same chain rope to the others on the Ora Hill; but if there was sufficient solid ground to stay on, they would not return; and in that case, Oodua and his other Chiefs should follow them by means of the same chain rope, so as to know where their predecessors were.

Accordingly, when Oodua and his other followers waited for a long time and did not see their predecessors return, they too descended; and eventually, they all reached a part of Ile-Ife called Mo-ore quarter at night. Till this day, the occasion of their entering the town at night is yearly celebrated by the idol worshippers, chief among whom are the Ifa priests of Ile-Ife.

On account of Orunmila and Obatala's preceding Oodua to Ile-Ife in the way just described, the descendants of Obatala continue till today claiming that their ancestor, Obatala, preceded Oodua to Ile-Ife with the sole object of coming to found Ile-Ife. They turn the matter to mean that Obatala was the first man commissioned by the Lord of Heaven to go and found the Ife town; but when he came near the town, he got drunk of palmwine and fell asleep. Consequently, when Oodua, who came after him met him where he was fast asleep, he robbed him of the "Igba-Iwa" which he was carrying down to carve his town with. On the success of Oodua in getting the "Igba-Iwa" he eventually became the founder of Ife town, they say. Nevertheless, this point will be better dealt with when we come to the quarrel between Oodua and Obatala in this history.

When Oodua went back to Oke-Ora to stay, Obatala Ooyelagbo was acting in his place as the head of all. As it took a long time before things were done in such a way as to make the town to be worthy of its name, Obatala, as the head of all, had made an indelible good impression on the minds of a great number of people, so much so that they hardly had respect for any other person beside him, although they all were quite aware that Oodua, as their true King was yet coming.

When everything was ready, Ejio was sent to go and call Oodua according to the previous arrangement. It was on this account that many Ifes took it to mean that Ejio was the one whom the ancient Ifes sent to heaven, that is, (Oke-Ora) to get chieftaincies for them, because there was not a single chieftaincy at Ile-Ife until Oodua came the second time as a true King, who had the unquestionable right of giving out titles.

Learning that everything had been orderly arranged Oodua descended again by means of the same rope of chain at a place very near Ife City. The day of his royal entry was so grand that it is till today commemorated on the Coronation Day of every new Ooni. On that day, Chief Ejio was the one who escorted Oodua to the City through a circuitous route, which has since that time become the one which every new Ooni has to take to his palace on his coronation day. That is why it has since that time become the compulsory duty of Chief Ejio to be the usher of every new Ooni in on the day of his coronation, when Ejio has to say to the new Ooni thus – "This is the way which my father Orafioye took to meet your father Oodua on his royal entry into this City".

This thing was the one referred to, when Gerald Massey said, "Ife was in existence long before the traditional arrival of Oduduwa, for it is recorded that he was accepted by the people of Ife."

The two important messages carried by Chief Ejio to Oodua eventually conferred on him the honour of being one of the two men who have right to hold the sword of state with the Ooni during the Olojo Festival. The three men holding the swords were (1) Oshogun, whose duty it is to worship the Ogun (2) Ejio as the state messenger whom the people sent to usher Oodua in, and (3) Ooni as the true representative of Oodua. This is done till today.

These facts strongly call the attention of the readers

to the following outstanding facts –

(1) If Ooni was originally a slave, and not one of the true sons of Oodua, it will not be the imperative duty of every Ejio on the Coronation day of every new Ooni to say "This is the way which Orafioye my father took to meet your father Oodua on the day of is royal entry." If any Ejio happened to say so wrongly, the Ifes would have corrected him because he would not be there alone.

(2) On the other hand, if the Yoruba capital had been removed from Ile-Ife to Oyo as many people wrongly believe it, Alaafin or Owa of Ilesa, would have long been the real Oba to whom that open confession should have been periodically made instead of Ooni. This should have been so, since no rightful Alaafin has ever omitted getting his sword of state from the Ooni till today.

It was on account of what has been previously said that some people believe that, it is apparent that Oodua instituted a new dynasty. Nevertheless, the notable facts deduceable from this opinion of others are – (a) If Oodua was a new entrant and unpreviously known person to the Ifes, who did not hear anything about him before, instead of accepting his as their King, they would have offered him a very strong and heavy fighting. (b) It would not have been easy for Oodua to reign over the people about whom he did not hear or, know anything before. (c) The Ifes would not have sent someone to escort an unknown person into their town, where the new man would deprive them of many of their former privileges. (d) On the other hand, if Oodua did not return to Oke Ora so that he might eventually re-enter the city the second time in a state of royalty, not only would there would there have been no royal custom to be followed by his descendants after him as it is today, but also there would have been no difference between him and the ordinary people, and consequently, no one would have been serving the other as it used to be between a king and his people.

Oodua's Descent

The idea of the Ifes that Oodua descended from Ora Hill to Ile-Ife makes many people hold the view that Oodua was a mythical King. To rebut this notion, it may be pointed out that, it has never been known in any history that a human being actually descended from heaven. It has never on the other hand, been told of any spirit to have come to this world, not only to live among the people of the world, but also to rule over them as it was in the case of Oodua.

But here is Oodua, who was known, called and accepted, not only as a king, but also as the accredited progenitor of the whole Yoruba race.

The belief of many writers today that Oodua was a Myth, does not now remain with him alone, but it has been extended to both Oranmiyan and Ile-Ife respectively. Consequently, they call Oodua and Oranmiyan, mythical kings; and Ile-Ife, "legendary cradle" of the Yoruba race as well as that of the whole universe.

Today, it is read in history books that, there is not in the world any real Hausa Stock; and yet, it is universally accepted that the Hausa language is still living and spoken by millions of people. Hitherto, it has not been told when various invaders came to wipe the original Hausas out of the surface of the earth.

What is definitely known about the Hausas are: (1) that there were seven original Hausa states, *viz.*, Kano, Rano, Zegzeg (Zaria), Daura, Gobir, Katsena and Zamfara; and that to them were afterwards added the Hausa Banza, who were perhaps in the minority. (2) That some of the written Hausa records, and not the Hausas themselves, were systematically destroyed by their Fulani conquerors, especially Bello, the learned first Sultan of Sokoto. The conquest of the Fulani over the Hausas, and the systematic destruction of the latter's written records did not start in the right sense until after Bello was made the Sultan of Sokoto in 1808, by his father Usuman dan Fodio.

Although the Hausas used to fight one another for supremacy before the Fulani rose to power, yet, it was never known that they entirely destroyed one another; and no history has shown when, why and how the Hausas were annihilated. Heaven then knows how the modern historians arrived at the conclusion which prompted them to say "No original Hausa stock exists in the world today."

The Yoruba people are known and recognized in every part of the world today as existing; nevertheless, their ancestors are now regarded as myths, and their land of common origin is also regarded "A legendary cradle of the Yoruba race." If, therefore, due and sufficient care is not taken by us, the time will soon come, when the history of Ile-Ife will be like that of Hausaland. It is then likely to be said of the Ifes thus – "Although Yoruba language is still living and spoken by millions of people today, yet, there is not original Ife stock in existence." This is certainly sure to be so, so long as Oodua and Oranmiyan their ancestors are taken to be mere myths.

Now, coming back to the real point at issue, that if Oodua came to live in this world in the form of a spirit, it may be said certainly that he was nothing but an actual mythical man and King; and cannot be the progenitor of our Obas, because a spirit cannot be either. If on the other hand, he was an undeniable King and progenitor of the whole Yoruba race, then, he was not a spirit; and consequently, was not a mythical, but a real King.

If the idea that Oodua was the father of all the Obas of our whole country is within the Ife area alone, one will be tempted to say that such a thought is purely unfounded;

but it is a happy thing to say that there is not a part of our whole country in which the genuine fatherhood of Oodua to all our Obas and people has ever been doubted or denied. The open and hearty acceptance of this truth by all our Obas indicates that Oodua was really once a man and king as they themselves are, and not a spirit.

A question may here arise thus – "If Oodua was actually a man and King and not a spirit, how did he manage to be in existence?" Yes, the answer to this question is not far to seek. According to the Watt Catechism, used in all C.M.S. Schools, people are given to understand that Adam was the first created man of God, and he was the father of us all. The expression, "First made by God, almost imply that somebody else was afterwards made by God, when the Epistle to the Hebrews, chapter 7, verses 1-3 running thus, is compared with this – "For this Melchisedec, King of Salem, priest of the Most High God, who met Abraham returning from the slaughter of the Kings and blessed him. To whom also Abraham gave a tenth part of all; first being by interpretation, King of righteousness and after that, also King of Salem, which is, Kin of Peace; without father, without mother, without descent, having neither beginning of days, nor end of life; made like unto the Son of God, abideth a priest continually."

Like Oodua, Melchisedec referred to here was not a mere commoner, but was the King of Salem; still, he was reported to be without father, without mother, without descent, having neither beginning of days, nor end of life; but was made like unto the Son of God.

All human beings, including Jesus Christ, were, and are still born and not made; but this man, Melchisedec was said to be made in the same way as Adam was, and not born.

God causes rain to fall and the sun to shine alike in

every part of the globe, except in the extreme cold and extreme dry regions. He causes these two important life-giving elements as well as the most vital life sustaining and greatest element – the air to operate in every part of the extensive world. It is therefore, not surprising to hear that the same God, Who made, and not born Adam, made Melchisedec in another place and at another time; so also could He have found it fit and feasible for Him to make and not born Oodua, somewhat round about the Ora Hill, and subsequently to have him descended at Ile-Ife.

It is a universally admitted and undeniable fact, that there is no impossibility in God's dictionary. He can make and unmake any number of persons or things at will; and there is nobody to query His Action.

Nobody knows the exact place where either Adam or Melchisedec was made, and how he reached the place where he lived. Therefore, the fact that we did not witness Oodua actually descending does not strongly make it sufficient reason why we should regard him a mythical, or legendary King, or fabulous ancestor of the whole of our race.

In like manner, there is no thly hly-reasonable ground for anyone to call or regard Oranmiyan the most powerful and war-like of all the Oonis of Ife, a mythical King.

In another part of this history, readers will see how it has been clearly proved that when Oranmiyan reigned as the Ooni of Ife, and not as Alaafin of Oyo, one of his sons, Eweka I, was the King of Benin. Equally so has it been proved that at the same time, another one of his sons – Ajaka, reigned as the Alaafin of Oyo and another at Ife. If therefore, Oranmiyan is taken and regarded as a myth, will the Ooni of Ife, who sits directly on the ancient throne, handed over from Oodua to Obalufon-Ogbodirin, from Obalufon to Oranmiyan , etc., the Oba of Benin, and the Alaafin of Oyo, who are the direct offsprings of

Oranmiyan, not be regarded as Mythical Kings in future?

On the other hand, if the mentioned ones are regarded as actual men, then, Oodua and Oranmiyan were actually men too.

HOW THESE FACTS ARE KNOWN

It is self-evident that however long the time of the birth of a person may be, and however far the place of his birth is, from where he was brought up, it is not feasible that the memory of such important things will be lost entirely by everybody; and more especially when a reasonably large number of people are concerned in the matter of birth at a particular place.

If the people born at a special place were very young when they were removed from their place of birth to go and stay somewhere else, there will not altogether be lacken a few elderly people who will one way or the other mention to the young people, the name of the place of their birth; but where, for hundreds of years together, no mention of a different place of birth other than the one in which they live is made to a group of people, definitely, it will mean that such people are in their true place of birth.

This was exactly the condition in the case of Oodua and his people who, till the end of their earthly journeys, could not trace their place of origin beyond Oke-Ora, from where they came to Ile-Ife. Their coming to Ile-Ife was so curious and astounding to the people of the world afterwards that they considered Oke-Ora and Ile-Ife as north and lower heaven respectively. This was what Gerald Massey referred to in his book page 601, Volume Ii, when he said thus – "In the Yoruba Mythology, Ile-Ife is a region of north (Oke-Ora) or lower (Ile-Ife) heaven out of which the sum issues forth and is reborn from his burial place".

This assertion goes without saying, with a part of what was referred to earlier as being common belief of the whole of our people before some writers came to say that our ancestors came originally from Mecca or Egypt thus – "(1) "Ile-Ife, the land of ancient days (2)"Ile-Ife, from where the dawn of day was first seen".

It is, above all, very significant that, up till today, there has never been any person in the whole of our vast country that has once traced his origin, or origin of anything he or she does to Egypt or any of the other places assumed by other writers as the original home of the Yorubas as they do to Ile-Ife.

Oodua's Followers

Another very immensely important things causing much unrest of mind among readers are, how and from where Oodua got his followers.

This question is apparently beyond all human comprehension; nevertheless, it seems that their making was in all probability like that of the people of nod, about whom we read in the Book of Genesis, Chapter IV, verses 16 and 17 thus – "And Cain went out from the presence of the Lord, and dwelt in the land of Nod, on the east of Eden.

"And Cain knew his wife; and she conceived, and bare Enoch; and he builded a city, and called the name of the city after the name of his son Enoch".

At first, Adam and the members of his family were the only known people living on earth; but after the death of Abel, the wrath of God came upon Cain, who killed his more faithful brother than himself, and consequently, he ran away into the land of nod, about which no one had heard or known anything before that time. The most astounding part of the story is, not only did Cain take refuge in the land of nod, but he even married and got a child there, whereas it was nowhere previously mentioned that

Cain had a wife from among his sisters if he had any at all, or from anywhere else before he ran to that place. This almost make it very plain that, when Adam and his family were living separately in a part of the world, another group of people, curiously made by God, were living elsewhere in the world. Were there no people in that place before that time, Cain would not have gone there with the strong purpose of taking refuge.

The most extensive desert in Africa, the Sahara, with its length of 3,000 miles and its breadth of 1,000 miles, is everywhere admitted to be a rainless piece of land. Nevertheless, not only are there a number of fertile pieces of land, called "Oases", where people live and get water there, but one can hardly go beyond a distance of 300 miles before one comes to a well full of water.

If God could make all these things to the advantage of His creatures, would it be impossible for Him to create Oodua and his followers separately before he brought them together for the first time on Ora Hill?

It must be called to mind that, it was on the same hill that Oodua first saw the five fingered fowl which he eventually sent to spread the magical sand already referred to.

That Oodua was ile-Ife and Ile-Ife was Oodua has, from time immemorial, made all the tribes of our land to accept him as their genuine progenitor, and Ile-Ife, as their true place of common origin.

OKE-ORA

One of our native sayings runs thus – "Whatever no eye has ever seen, is a don't of the eyes."

When our great great grandparents were told that not only Oke-Ora was considered the earthly dwelling house of Oramife, and the place from where Oodua and his sixteen elders descended to found the city of Ife, they did not realize the appallingness of those stories until many years afterwards.

It was related that one day a poor and needy hunter shot a stag at the foot of this Ora Hill. It immediately fell down as if it were dead. When the hunter drew near with a view to laying his hand on it, the stag suddenly rose up and began to run away. Thinking that it would soon fall down again, he rigorously followed the half dead stag until he came to a place very near the summit of the hill. There, he unexpectedly came to a very broad, long and straight road in a very thick forest. It is said that the scene was so pathetic to the hunter that he fearfully ran back without telling the story to anyone.

Several months after, another more courageous hunter, who was closely related to the first one shot another at a different place at the foot of the same hill. Curious enough, his shot stag did exactly the same thing as done by that of the previous hunter. In following its blood strained path, the second hunter came to the same broad, long and very clean road as seen by the former hunter. Being fearless, he waited for a few minutes to think about this unexpected wonderful road. While he was doing this, he saw a large number of pigeons, fowls, dogs and goats. In the end, the hunter became so horror stricken that he took to his heels and ran back home. Believing that as a consequence of what he saw, he would die, he began to tell people what he saw on the Ora Hill, so that elderly people might help him out of his trouble. When the first man learnt of his purpose of telling other people, he also gave the report of his own experience on the same hill.

To prove the authenticity of the stories of those hunters, a body of people were purposely sent to go and verify what they saw, but neither road, nor domestic animal or bird was seen. Consequently, no credence was attached to their stories.

Although for very many years the stories of those two hunters were not accepted as being true, yet, when, owing to the war which broke Ile-Ife on the 20th of October, 1882, the Ifes in their flight left the town, they also could not take with them any of their domestic animals. One of the places they went to make temporary abodes was Shaga, at the foot of Ora Hill. The story was told that after staying at that place for some time, several of them began to see curious dogs and goats coming to stay with them. At first, they did not know from where the dogs and goats came to stay with them; but in course of years they began to have puppies and kids. Later on, it was observed that, in all cases without a single exception, when the young ones were old enough to be separated from their mothers, both the mothers and the young ones used to be missed for days together; but later on, the mothers with half of the young ones would return as the shares of the persons who had been feeding them.

When this practice continued for a long time, the caretakers began to watch their dogs and goats so as to know what used to happen to the young ones which used to stay away when about a half of them with the mothers would come back to them. Eventually, they found that the dogs with their puppies used to go to an unknown person on the Ora Hill for impartial division of the puppies whey they were old enough for distribution. This was why many elderly people said afterwards that most of the dogs which the Ifes brought back home after the war were sent to them by Oramife from Ora Hill.

Till some forty or forty five years ago, this story was so common among the elderly Ife people that everybody regarded their unforced story as accurate as Oke-Ora itself was wonderful and mysterious.

This appalling provision of some domesticated animals to the Ifes whey they were in dire need of such animals makes the whole Ifes believe firmly till today in the descent of Oodua and his followers from the same hill, to found the city of Ile-Ife.

Now, with the great outstanding discovery of Dr. Leakey, and the examination and sentence which the selected fifty scientist delegates of the world have unanimously passed on his finds, that Africa was the home of man in making, it is hoped that permanent stoppage will be put to the argument in favour of Asia as being our place of origin. Then it may stand to reason that the dark skinned Sumerians who first lived in the valleys of Rivers Tigris and Euphrates, the wild tribes, who came from north-west to conquer them, the black people who were the second group of the people to live in Britain before the Celtics, who preceded the Britons, and the Black fellows of Australia, were some of the negroes who went out of Africa to found those places. Therefore, the vital question which now remains for the world scientists to settle is, what part of Africa in which man truly first started to live, because the stories of both Egypt and East Africa, where relics of ancient people were found, one thing is prominently lacken, and that one thing is, "Mixture of fair skinned people and the negroes" as was reported to be found at Ile-Ife.

THE SIXTEEN ELDERS
THAT CAME WITH OODUA TO ILE-IFE

The following were the sixteen elders that came with Oodua to found the city of Ile-Ife –

1. Orunmila, otherwise called Agbonniregun or Ifa.
2. Obatala-Ooyelagbo, otherwise called Orisala
3. Oluo-orogbo

4. Obameri, otherwise called, Alapa-Aharemada
5. Ore-Luere
6. Obasin
7. Obagede
8. Ogun
9. Obamakin
10. Obawinni
11. Aje
12. Erisile
13. Elesije
14. Olose
15. Alajo
16. Esidale.

Orunmila was the chief adviser of these first ruling bodies of Ile-Ife in all matters. Obatala was their head artist, and Oluorogbo was his next man in rank. Obameri was the general Elesije was the chief physician. Ogun was the chief hunter, and Aje was the banker or financier. Others were given various sanitary appointments for the removal of the dead bodies of people who died of being killed by fallen trees, fallen walls, dropping from palm trees, or the dead bodies of hunchbacks, cripples, albinos, and women who died in state of pregnancy.

How Ile-Ife Got its name

Originally, the arrangement of the coming of the elders down by means of a chain rope was mainly between Orunmila and Oodua; but before the latter returned to stay on the Ora Hill, until everything was ready for his royal arrival, his people wanted to know what the name of their town would be. In order that Oodua might be able to answer the cogent question rightly, he had to consult Orunmila.

On consulting his oracle, Orunmila declared that the finding of suitable name for their prospective town was not the exclusive work of a single person; but it was one that required a strong team work of the whole lot of them. He said that his oracle wanted them all to think deeply and bring out as many names as they possibly could for the approval of the oracle. Accordingly, they all started to think out names, after several fruitless attempts, one of the low ranking members among them suggested, "Ile Fe-e loju si I" which was the nickname they had long given to Oodua, when he used to say to that five fingered fowl, spreading the sand, and to their greatest surprise, this name was the most acceptable to the oracle as eventually declared by Orunmila.

As a result of this, Orunmila gave the result of consulting his oracle in the following words – "Omode iri ogbon, Agba a ma a ri ogbon ni ki a fi da Ile-Ife". That is why, it has from time immemorial passed into a saying thus – "Omode ir'ogbon, Agba'rogbon ni a fi da'le 'fe".

By this, Orunmila said that the oracle wanted them all always to be co-operative in the management of the town.

As brevity has from time immemorial been necessary in a number of things, in course of time, the name of the time was by degrees contracted to "Ile'fe"; but as Oodua alone could not spread as many people would, his people considered themselves worthy of being called spreading people too; and hence, they all claimed to be known as "Ifes", and consequently, the name of their town became "Ile-Ife", as they are today.

Quarrel Between Oodua and Obatala

Originally, from the nature of his work as the one who was believed to fashion men and women, after the Great

166

Lord of heaven had created human beings, Obatala was considered next to the Creator. Though he was not made a king as Oodua, yet, when Oodua had not come down the second time, he was the head of the other people. He wisely caused the people to add one of his appellations "O-Oye-lagbo", to that of Oodua, in the name of the city. That is why, until this day, we sometimes hear people say, "Ile-Ife O-Oye lagbo."

By this expression, Obatala had craftily turned "Ile-Ife to his own, according to Oodua's concept. When Oodua knew this thing on his arrival the second time, he tried to dissuade Obatala from the continuation of such a compound name, but Obatala eventually proved so fastidious that he one day suddenly rose up against Oodua.

When the latter, who was not prepared for such an attack could no longer resist the aggressive manner of the former, he and his people did as little as they could before they took to their heels and left the palace and its precincts in terror.

Before that time, the dwelling place of Obatala was "Idita-Ile" at Igbotapa, at a place between Ilode and Okerewe quarters of Ife. The then dwelling place of Obameri was the exact place where the present Saint Paul Church, Ayegbaju of the C.M.S., is today, at a place between Ijio and Ilode. Though Obameri's town house is today used as a Church and a school premises, yet, Obatala's town and country houses are still today used and called "Idita-Ile and Idita-Oke" respectively.

When Obameri heard that Obatala drove Oodua out of his palace, he promptly rose up in arms against Obatala. The latter was so completely conquered that he was eventually driven out of town. Consequently, Obatala went to a place now called "Idita-Oko", named after his town house to make his temporary abode. In order to aggravate the feeling of Obatala all the more, Obameri also moved out of the town to a place about one and half miles to where Obatala built his house, to build his own on the same road but his was much nearer to the town than that of Obatala; mainly to prevent the latter from molesting Oodua's peace in the town. On account of this, Obatala's people had to obtain Obameri's permission before they could come to buy their most needed things in the town.

The sites of the houses which those two important personalities built then are till today at places a little beyond Esinmirin stream on the way to Mokuro stream, from where the water drunk at Ile-Ife today is drawn.

The sole object of Obameri in removing to his country home was not only to prevent Obatala from attacking Oodua again but also to place Obatala under perpetual disgrace, for his insubordination and arrogancy. For this reason, although a few of the followers of Obatala were allowed to buy their food supplies from the town, yet, for years, Obameri did not allow Obatala and his important followers to enter the town. This high and touching deprivation of vital privileges made Obatala and his high ranking men took Obameri to be their sworn enemy.

This deprivation of privileges made many of Obatala's people become wanderers in the bush. By so doing, they were able to know various places and things which they could use to advantage whether they remained permanently in the bush or were allowed to return to the town.

After staying in their country houses for many years, some influential people in the town made a solid arrangement for settling the quarrel between Oodua and Obatala. In order that the whole matter might not prove abortive, Obameri was first seen and taken into confidence.

From time immemorial, Obatala, as a serious thinking artist, had no taste for palmwine; and so also was Oluorogbo. On the other hand, Obameri, as a warrior, could not at all do without taking palmwine any day.

According to the previous arrangement, on the day fixed for the settlement of the matter, Obatala and Obameri came home; but in order to play a practical joke on Obatala, before Obameri left for the town, he had instructed some of his servants to bring a big gourd of unadulterated palmwine to the side of the road after many hours they had gone to the town.

After everything had been properly settled, both Obameri and Obatala returned together to their country houses, chatting heartily as they came along; but suddenly, when they got near Obameri's house, he quickly outran Obatala as if he was going to take something out of his house before Obatala reached there. When it remained only a few yards before Obatala reached Obameri's house, the latter ordered one of his servants to break the gourd of undiluted palmwine on the road which Obatala had to pass. The pool of palmwine was so much that Obatala had to pass. The pool of palmwine was so much that Obatala had no alternatives than to wade it in displeasure. He later said, "Emu ki iti ese ipa orisa." This means that the mere wading through a pool of palmwine could not make him become drunk.

It is particularly worthy of notice that since that time, till even date, it has been the annual practice of the offsprings of Obameri during "Odun-Itapa" to run quickly to go and break a gourd of palmwine on the very spot where Obameri ordered the first gourd to be broken. Equally so have the offsprings of Obatala since then made it a point of duty to run as quickly as they could to pass that point before the worshippers of Obameri fill the place with a large pool of palmwine. If on the whole, the followers of Obameri had poured palmwine on the road before those of Obatala reached there, the latter would wade through the pool of palmwine with the added "Emu ki iti ese ipa Orisa" which Obatala used in the first instance.

Each year, during Itapa Festival till today, both sides always greet each other with series of abusive songs as their foreparents did in olden days, as soon as the point of contention is passed over either with the wading, or without wading through a pool of palmwine. Similarly, is the occasion of the fight between Obameri and Obatala yearly observed during the same period, by a number of hunters carrying their guns to watch the town gate leading to where one side will be trying to outrun the other in order that the road might be filled with palmwine, and the other will be trying to outrun his opponent, in order to avoid passing through a pool of palmwine.

ORIGIN OF THE IGBOS

After necessary settlement had been effected between Obatala and Obameri, Oodua asked them to evacuate their country houses for their former town houses. This royal order was promptly obeyed. Nevertheless, many of Obatala's wild boys were not willing to let Obameri and his people go unpunished one way or the other. Although they knew that this could not be done without punishing other people too, yet, they insisted on carrying out their tendentious purpose.

As many of them were hunters, who had been used to hard forest life when they were not allowed to come to town, as soon as they reached home, they left the town in pretence that they went a-hunting. During that time, they secretly made a circuitous bush-path through thick forests until they came to a place, known afterwards as "Igbo'gbo", that is, Igbo's Forest.

This place is very far from the town, and is almost

diametrically opposite to both town and their former country houses. The place where both Obatala and Obameri built their country houses is till this day on the right hand side of the road leading from Ile-Ife to Ilesa, while Igbo'gbo is on the left hand side of the road, leading from Ile-Ife through Isoya to Ijebuland.

Finding that place suitable for their tendentious purpose, they came back home to organize a secret society to which they gave the name "Igbo". For years together, they continued to carry on their hunting along with the secret society. At that time, it was a common practice for hunters to stay in the forest for two or more years together before coming home.

Whenever they went into the bush, they used to go to this "Igbo'gbo" to prepare it for the main purpose they had founded it. At first, it was used as the Oro worshippers use their "Igboro" for the sole worship of Oro, or as the Egungun worshippers use their "Igbale" mainly for the worship of Egungun.

Little by little, these hunters began to increase in number and little by little, they began to stay in the bushes much longer than ever before; but as the others were not in the know of their revengeful and wicked purpose, no one attached any importance to their absence from home.

When every serious memory of the fighting between Obatala and Obameri had almost been entirely lost to a reasonable extent, some of the members of the Igbo Secret Society moved to stay in their newly carved settlement, quite unknown to the other non members. There, they began to plan how best they could make their presence effectively but secretly felt in the town in order that they might be able to punish Obameri's followers. Obatala is till this day called Oba-Igbo because his followers started Igbo cult. This is another proof that the Igbos were real Ifes.

How Their Name Was Come About

It may be asked how they came about their name Igbos, and why they adopted it. The reason was that, those hunters being professional men, they had known the general habits and behaviours of several animals and birds whose habit they had known quite well was the one called "Igbo". This type of bird was everywhere known for its unequalled power and tactics of fighting among birds. Consequently, any group of birds which happened to find an Igbo in their midst would quickly disperse; otherwise, any of them that was a bit sluggish would instantly be mercilessly treated. That is why we have from time immemorial had that saying in our country thus – "Igbo wonu eye k'eyetu". This expression was often used for any person who is very fond of creating quarrel between two persons.

They adopted this fighting name to indicate what their attitude would be towards other peaceful towns people.

Like every other deceptive secret cults, the Igbos adopted a coat of fibre woven dress to cover themselves completely from head to ankles, leaving a small opening for their eyes to see through. For their offensive attack, they had a cudgel called "Igbon", and for their peaceful gesture, they had a round headed wooden object called "Suku". To whomsoever they stretched the Suku, it meant, they were at peace with such a person.

When every arrangement was perfectly made solid, the Igbos began to make their periodical raids on the town's people in a distinguishing manner through the circuitous roads previously mentioned.

In their journey through the forest, they used to travel as any earthly person would do under the same circumstances. Their disguising dress used to be carried on their heads until they came very near to Esinmirin Stream, just a few minutes' walk to the town on the same

172

road, where Obatala and Obameri's country house are. This same road leads to the Mokuro Stream, now drawn to the Ife City for drinking purpose. Here each used to put on his curiously looking dress, which made the ancient people consider them to be people celestial whom no terrestrial people had a right to see without being dead.

The people were so clever that the end of their circuitous road to the main road was not one, but were so many that no other person was aware that some particular persons used to come through them to the main road. Consequently, whenever the cunning Igbos made their deceiving appearance, the Ifes used to run away. More terror was strongly stricken into the minds of the deceived ones from the fact that, not a single one of the caught ones ever returned to the town. The cardinal belief of everyone was that those who had been captured had been carried to heaven.

From time immemorial, not only men but majority of women know that neither Egungun nor Oro comes from heaven, yet, till today men usually spend heavy money during the Egungun Festival and are even highly delighted in calling Egunguns celestial beings; how much more are women who are very credulous?

In like manner, though many of the town's people as members of the Igbos in the town knew everything about the doings of the Igbos, yet, they did not reveal their secret; therefore, the merciless practice continued for a long time unchallenged. Eventually some seriously thinking people who thought that such frequent molestation of the peace of every individual had become so intolerable that it should not be left indefinitely unchallenged, began very earnestly to think about how to go about the matter without losing their lives and homes in the anxious period. Then it became the unpleasant question of "Who will bell the cat?"

One of the people mostly concerned in such a deep

thought about the welfare of their people more than that of their own was a very beautiful and highly patriotic woman named Moremi.

Later on, this woman, who had only one son named Ela, came to be in forefront of all the people wishing to know how to put an end to the frequent and wasteful activities of their unwanted guests.

This woman set herself to the heavy task of finding out very secretly whether those who had from time to time been troubling her people were really heavenly or earthly beings. While she was going in search of this uncertain truth, somebody who had a slight knowledge of the secret cult of the Igbos, told her that he firmly believed that their molesters were not celestial, but terrestrial beings as they themselves were.

Hearing this, Moremi sat down quietly for hours together, thinking very seriously on how the fact of what she had heard could be drawn out. Eventually, it strongly occurred to her to go and consult Ifa oracle for the testimony of what she had heard. On consultation, Ifa oracle boldly corroborated what she had been partially told.

On hearing this, a very stricken idea quickly haunted her. The idea was, her very stout resolution of wishing herself to be caught by an Igbo, as one of their easily caught preys, so that she might have an ample opportunity of understudying their general ways of life. Pondering over this seemingly bright thought still profoundly, she became puzzled about how she could best implement her project. When she did not know what else to do, she again went to her former Ifa priest to help her out of her disturbing state of mind.

On consulting Ifa oracle, the priest asked her to give a hearty thank to a stream of water thrice for the impeding wonderful victory that would presently be hers through the assistance of the god of that stream. In addition, the priest told her that she would have to make a promise of giving a valuable gift to the god of the stream, if she happened to find out their ways of life and conquer them.

So long as she had been promised of a sure and complete victory over the Igbos, she counted nothing too big for her to offer as a sacrifice unto the god of that stream if truly she could have the promised victory. Therefore, in order to make the grave situation doubly sure, she asked the Ifa priest to mention the particular thing she had to offer as an acceptable propitiation. The Ifa priest replied that there was nothing else than her own hearty promise. Thinking very deeply for a while, she said that she had no other thing to offer in sacrifice than whatever would first come from her house to meet her on her return, if she could go and return. The vow was unhesitatingly agreed to by the Ifa priest.

A few months after this rash vow had been made, the troublesome Igbos came in their customary manner, in a much greater number than ever before. But curious enough, when every other person was running helter skelter, Moremi remained almost motionless as if she was unconcerned. Eventually she presently became a proud slave of one of them.

Moremi was so beautiful that she soon became an every moment object of attraction to all Igbo raiders that came. Therefore, their leader strongly aimed at getting her for a wife from the one who captured her, exchanging her for another catch; nevertheless, the young officer would not give in. Consequently, no sooner they reached their bush house than the Igbo leader made their chief to understand that amongst the newly caught people there was a very charming woman in possession of one of the men of the expedition. On hearing this, the chief called for the man who captured Moremi and exchanged the woman with another one of less beauty. There and then Moremi became the woman of the highest rank at "Igbo'gbo".

For many months, she was as shy as any other humble and shameful woman might be. Therefore, in order to cheer her up, the husband, who had almost everything at his disposal, began to show her all the secret places, telling her all the private things about their secret cult. Eventually, he inadvertently told Moremi how that place was founded, and the object of their settling there. Further still, he told her about their method of raiding and what were their dos and don'ts. In short, the more these things were revealed to Moremi, the more she showed love to her new husband. The degree of their mutual love became so high that Moremi, more than any other woman, was allowed to move freely anywhere.

As none of the people previously captured and carried to that place had ever thought of going back home, and as Moremi had had more privileges than any other woman there, no one thought that she would have ever cherished any hope of running back home. Nevertheless, after she had gained adequate knowledge of their method of catching people, and what she could do to check their further incursions, she one day secretly left Igbo'gbo, almost naked, in order to avoid suspicion, she left almost all her things behind. Before they were aware of her escape, she had clean gone; and after much sufferings and dire needs she at length reached home.

On reaching the town gate, the people wishing to welcome her home were so many that she could hardly know one from the other. But it was very regrettable to note that immediately the news of her coming back was broken to the members of Moremi's household, her only son Ela, was the first to run and meet her. Nevertheless her joy was so full that she did not remember anything about her vow again.

When she reached home, she summoned all the elders together. In the meeting, she gave the full report of what led her to conclude that without being caught and carried into the camp of their oppressors, she would not be able to help them adequately. Further, she told them how she had so studied the Igbos' ways of molesting the peace of the Ifes at home, that she had found out that not only were they people from among them, but in their disguised dress, they could not stand the smallest spark of fire. In addition, she said that as she had escaped, their coming back upon the town's people would not be long and therefore, due defensive preparations should be made against them.

PREPARATION AGAINST THEM

It now became incumbent duty on every responsible person who was not in the secret society of the Igbos in the town to get together and find an effective way of checking the people whom they formerly believed to be heavenly beings. After series of secret meetings, the people arrived at the arrangement of making a special type of torches which would be able to stand the current of the wind to some extent. Later on, some of the more experienced men said that the torch of the mixture of a large quantity of tow and palm oil would be better than any other one.

Therefore, in order to avoid delay, arrangement was quickly made to fetch tow and good palm oil very profusely.

Next to this, when it was felt that the unfriendly visit of the Igbos was fast approaching, some hunters were sent to go and waylay them very near Esinmirin Stream. Each of those men was provided with a pot full of well beaten okro, mixed with sufficient water to give a very slippery form whenever anybody happened to tread on it. The arrangement was so made that the mixture used to be changed and replaced by another whenever it was noticed that it was giving away its slippery value owing to the non coming of the Igbos in time. Again in order that the men lying in bush might not feel unduly tired for not seeing the Igbos, to come in time, they too used to be replaced by another group of men from time to time.

The capital object of waylaying the Igbos was not in the main to give them any onset as soon as they were seen, but to split the mixture of the okro and water on the wooden bridge placed over the stream over which they had to pass after they should have gone to the city. In order that the mixture might not get dried before the Igbos returned, the people lying in wait were warned not to pour it on the bridge until they heard a great and unusual noise from the city. In addition to this, private sentinels were set in some other important places, so that the townspeople might know how to take to their heels in time by dragging the Igbos to where they would be properly hemmed in on all sides.

Finally, the men who would fight them with several lit torches already prepared were placed at Okoro's house, in a part of the King's market, called Erunwa till today.

One day, the crafty Igbos forcefully came in yet greater number than ever before, and the alert home sentinels, standing on all strategic points, promptly gave signals of their fast approaches.

At first, the town's people, who had been previously instructed how to deal with the grave situation, appeared as if they did not know that they were coming. Taking that as a fitting opportunity for an immense catch, the Igbos were coming in quick marches. After they had been drawn to the heart of the town, the apparent care free town's people began to run away helter skelter. Suddenly the torch bearers, called Agbenas till today emerged with their curious song of "Ero, ero, ero, Sere, ero, Sere. Oni-maku-maku Sere, ero sere", and pursued hotly after the Igbos in their strange woven and made fibre dress, and set fire to as many of them as they were able to overtake.

Seeing the horrible fate of the front group, the Igbos who were yet behind ran back. As soon as the people who had long been lying in bush heard an unusual terrible noise, they poured the mixture of water and okro which they had with them on the bridge over the Esinmirin Stream. As the Igbos did not leave the bridge in a wet and slippery condition when they were going, they did not hesitate to run pass it – but on the contrary, before they reached there, the bridge had become so wet and slippery that all of them that stepped it fell down topsy turvy into water below, and were carried away by the strong current.

In the town, many of those attacked by the torch bearers were instantly burnt to death; but a few of them who escaped from being burnt, took refuge at Aka's house, at the site of the present Ife General Mosque at Erunwa. The memory of their then flight used to be commemorated in that particular house until a serious offence against the late Ooni Ademiluyi, by a member of the house, caused the whole house to be evacuated. Nevertheless, the ceremony of carrying burning torches and of the captured Igbos running away from the torch bearers is still performed at Ile-Ife till today.

THE FINAL DESTRUCTION OF THE IGBOS

As it had clearly been known that those who formed the Igbo secret society before they went curiously to go and settle at "Igbo'gbo" were the same Ifes as the Ifes of the town; and still they were so hard hearted as to bring such a calamity as they had experienced upon them all, the town's people were unanimous on the destruction of the responsible Igbos. Consequently, a very strong punitive expedition was arranged against Igbo'gbo with a view to retrieving as many of the captives carried there as possible, and destroying the ring leaders of the Igbos. But as the Igbos in their country home had learned of the fate of the men they had sent to raid the town, before the Ifes at home got ready for Igbo'gbo, a great many of the Igbos had left their country home and had gone in various directions.

As the forest in which they lived then led to several Ijebu farm lands, some of the Igbos escaped into what is known as Ijebu part today. Not only did they settle in various parts of this place, but their chiefs who ranked next to Obatala as their king, actually settled there, and they were the very people who went to settle at Ijebu-Ode in various waves before Ogborogan, who was one of the real sons of Oodua, went to settle there.

As they used to come to Ile-Ife town by way of Ilesa, when on their last raid they were attacked at Esinmirin Stream, majority of them fearfully ran to Ilesa part; and they were the people whom Atakumasa, Owa of Ilesa, met at Ilesa when he reached there from Ibokun. It is said further that a group of them went to stay at Ijero in Ekiti land. In addition, it is related that some of them were so angry that they travelled as far as to the eastern part of Nigeria, where they are still known as the "Igbos" till this day.

If the Igbos' going to settle in other parts of Nigeria is not sure, still, that of Ijebu-Ode and districts is almost indisputably certain, because the "Jigbo", in form of the raiding Igbos in dress, and the Obirin-Ojowu, which they took there from their country home are still done there today. In like manner, the "Ebi" Festival done in memory of Moremi, carried there by Ogborogan, the first Awujale, is still done in many parts of Ijebu, where they call it "Ebi".

After the complete destruction of Igbo'gbo, a strong curse, like that which the Sultan of Sokoto pronounced on one of his villages called "Satiru" in 1906, was pronounced by the then reigning Ooni that no one should live at that place again.

As a fulfillment of that curse, stories were told by some yet living hunters that, during the closing period of the nineteenth century, that wild rubber was allowed to be tapped freely, no hunter or a rubber tapper could spend a night peacefully at Igbo'gbo. It was related that during the night, various fetish songs of the type of those used by the Ifes at home, used to be heard in several places, sung by unseen people. It was said that, sometimes, it would appear that the unseen people with their heartrending songs were almost on the same spot where the hunters, or rubber tappers were. The condition used always to be so deplorable that the place was for many years abandoned. It was the rapid method of cocoa growing of recent years that moved a reasonably large number of people to go in a strong body to make farms at Igbo'gbo with impunity as things are today.

MEMORY OF THE DISASTER ON BOTH SIDES

During the crushing expedition of the home people to Igbo'gbo, not only were many of the culprits put to death, but a few of them were brought home to be taught a practical object lesson. Therefore, after everything had become quite smooth on all sides, the Ifes at home chose from amongst the arrested Igbos the following to be chiefs amongst their remaining people – (1) Obawinrin; (2) Obarena; (3) Obariyun and (4) Woyeasiri. Obalara, who wears the same dress with them was mainly made their warden.

The capital purpose of choosing these chiefs was two folds, namely (1) to make the remaining Igbos remember continually the amount of evil which their people had caused to happen on both sides. (2) That the Ifes at home might be able to perpetuate the memory of how the Igbos were eventually overcome completely in the town and in the country. For this reason, each year, till today, the torch bearers have to hide themselves in a part of the palace where the first torch bearers hid themselves against the last wave of the Igbos. Equally so have the chiefs mentioned above to run helter skelter to Aka's house on a side of Erunwa Market, where their predecessors first took refuge when the torch bearers came out against them.

The common name for the Igbos at Ile-Ife today is "Oluyare". The name was originally derived from these words – (a) Olu, or "Eniti", that is, he who (b) Yin, which in Ife tongue means take protection of. For instance, if an elderly person wants to punish a boy or a girl for an offence committed, if the offender is lucky to get another elderly person nearby, he or she will quickly run to catch hold of such a person with the loud cry of "Mo yin lagbaja", that is, I seek protection under the person named; and as a mark of respect for that person, the pursuer will immediately cease following the offender.

(3) Are, in Ife language means the most ancient and honoured Crown which the Ooni inherited from Oodua. The Crown was so esteemed in ancient time that it was regarded as the highest thing with which any person could take an oath on any matter of importance with the desired effect; and, therefore, whatever might be the nature of any person's offence, so long as he was able to say "Bi mo ba se nkan yi ki Are mu mi", that is, If I am guilty of this offence, may I be punished by the Crown, he would be set free immediately; because it was firmly believed that if such a person was guilty he was sure to suffer the consequence as the name of the oldest, and most honoured Crown, was connected with it.

In like manner, if any person said "Mo yin Are", or "Mo fi Are be o", that is, I seek protection under the Ooni's

Crown, in those days, he would be let alone.

Therefore, in order that the Igbos, who took refuge in Aka's house might prove that by the protection of the Crown which they sought in that house, they were spared, they consequently adopted the name of "Oluy'are Igbo", by which they are known today. This means, people who took refuge under the protection of the Crown.

FULFILMENT OF VOW

On account of the overjoyousness of the mammoth crowd of people that came to welcome Moremi on her return from Igbo'gbo, she temporarily forgot her promise to the deity of the Esinmirin Stream. When, on the other hand, she remembered, the real first thing that came from her house to meet her was not quite known to her; therefore, she made a profuse sacrifice of as many animals as she thought would be acceptable unto the god of the stream. After that, everybody was so satisfied and at ease that no hope of any other national mishap from any quarter was cherished.

Nevertheless, after a few years, an unusual thing occurred again at Ile-Ife. Without any heavy downpour of rain, it was one day suddenly seen that the bank of the Esinmirin Stream became so overflown that no one could go from one side of it to the other. Furthermore, it was within a few other days noticed that the progress of the deluge towards the town was appallingly far beyond all expectations, because its volume seemed to increase surprisingly daily.

The heavy pressure brought upon the whole Ifes was so severe and pernicious that they had to resort to consultation of Ifa oracle so as to know the cause of their horrible plight. In response, Ifa said that the sole cause of their national trouble was that, one of them had made an unfulfilled vow, and without the vow being made good, there could be no end to their trouble until the whole town was completely deluged.

On hearing this, Ifa was further consulted so as to know the particular person who was responsible for the unfulfilled promise, so that the onus of making it good might be made incumbent on him or her. In answer, Ifa declared Moremi as the culprit of the matter. When this news flashed to the ears of the great men of the town; they refrained from breaking such a sad piece of news to the hearing of Moremi. Nevertheless, the news reached her.

No sooner Moremi received the bad intelligence than she began to check up, so as to know where her fault was. Pondering over the matter deeply for a long time, she detected that her vow to the Esinmirin Stream was to offer to it anything that might first come out to meet her on her way back home if she could be privileged to know the secrecy of the Igbos, and yet live to return safely. Then she realized that none of the things she had previously offered in sacrifices was appropriate. Consequently, on further checking up, she was made to understand that her only son, Ela, was the person to run out to meet her on her return from Igbo'gbo. On hearing this, she was so taken aback that for a few minutes, she did not know what to do or say. However, a few more moments, she summed up courage to offer her only son as a sacrifice to the Esinmirin Stream in order that the whole Ife people might not perish.

When Moremi's decision came to the hearing of the people, they were not pleased; but owing to the impending danger that was hanging on them all, they could not entirely prevent her from carrying out her wish for their safety. Eventually, Ela, the only son of Moremi, was killed to propitiate the deity of Esinmirin Stream.

WHY MOREMI BECAME THE PERPETUAL ADOPTED MOTHER OF ALL IFES

After Ela's death, the whole Ifes went into a great mourning for the irreparable loss, not only because he was innocent of the offence for which he was slain, but because Moremi, who had done so much for them became a childless woman for the love she had for them all. Therefore, everyone of them heartily vowed from that day that they all, as well as their offsprings from generation to generation would stand as her sons and daughters as long as the world lasts. That is why Moremi is till this day known as "Yeye Aye gbogbo" (that is, Mother of all), by the Ifes.

EDI, AND NOT IDI FESTIVAL - ORIGIN OF

A day after Ela's death, the elders of the town sent some people to go and collect his corpse; but to their utter amazement, the corpse was entirely found missing. Some people said that Ela rose up and ascended into heaven; nevertheless, there was nothing to substantiate this as being authentic.

When all search for his dead body entirely proved futile, the Ifes thought of doing something which would made both Ela and his mother Moremi ever be remembered. Therefore, in order to make this meet the expectation of everybody, they created a feast, called "Edi", and not "Idi", as other writers would like to call it. Seven days were set aside for the observation of this feast. The first day of this feast, which is observed till today deals partly with the memory of the molestation of the Igbos on the town people; and partly with the death of Ela. Therefore, in order to give everybody full time to make due preparation for this feast, an interval of from 25 to 35 days is yearly given.

From the day that the date of celebrating Edi is announced, various songs of praise in honour of Moremi will be started singing by everybody on his or her way to and from farm, from the town gates to all farms and back to the same gates till a day preceding the actual day of celebration. From that first day till the seventh, various songs in praise of Moremi are usually sung by everybody in the town.

FERETEKE DAY

The eve of the celebration of Edi is called "FERETEKE" Day. This word "Ferekete" is a mere password used by a group of people known as "Owa, or Otu Agbebos". In olden days, they were the national sacrifice-carriers. It is their yearly duty to usher "Edi" in by resorting to a grove on the Mo-ore (now) Ife-Ilesa road for the preliminary ceremony on the eve of the Festival. From that place, they will be shouting "Ferekete" led by one of them, when the others will be answering, "Aye-e", throughout the town until about 4.30 a.m. throughout that period, no one has the right of seeing them, only their passwords are always heard.

OGUNNA OR OFONRAN DAY

The first day of the celebration is always as eventful as the seventh day. The two things observed on the first day are (a) Ogunna or Ofonran burning and throwing overhead, (b) Idana-Olori, or Isa-Igare.

It will be of interest to the readers to know that "Igare" is another name given to the Igbos in their wild state of life in their country home, where they were acting like climbing animals. They are still known by this name till today.

On the previous night, every head of a house (Baale)

186

will provide all the people under him with a log of a very hard wood called "Ita". This log will be split into small pieces, called "Ofonran", with a view to making fire with them very early next morning.

As Moore quarter was where Oodua and his people first settled on his cursory first visit to Ile-Ife, it has from time immemorial been the duty of the Obalurin of Mo-ore to usher Edi in, on that morning by shouting very loudly at about 4.30 a.m. or 5 a.m. thus - "Yo-o-Iku yo, Arun yo, Agbeleperi-eni yo, Awiy'oko yo, Awiy'odo yo, Eniwipe kin g mase t'emi yo".

As soon as he shouts thus, every Baale will wake up his people to put their small pieces of Ita wood into fire. When Obalurin of Mo-ore shouts the second time, each Baale will re-echo "Yo-O-yo", etc. then everybody from the oldest to the smallest will wake up carrying his or her two pieces of the split Ita wood, and shouting "Yo-o-yo", etc, as he or she goes until the frontage of the Baale's official house called "Akodi", is reached. There, the pieces of wood will be waved overhead by each one before he or she throws them down anyhow.

After all pieces of wood must have been dropped, some of the young men will be requested by the elders to collect all the pieces of the firewood, and make them into groups for burning to ashes as a sign of warding off the Igbos, that they might nevercome to trouble them again from wherever they had gone to.

All the elderly people must remain on the spot till the whole thing is entirely burnt into ashes. While they are watching the burning, the young and the little boys will be engaged in wrestling Leaving this place, every body will be engaged in eating, drinking and merriment of all kinds.

IDANA-OLORI OR ISA-IGARE

After sufficient eating and drinking, the young men of each quarter will form themselves into groups of fighters, going to another quarter on fighting tournaments. On reaching a quarter, they would challenge the young men of that quarter to wrestling contests, by singing thus, "K'elerekun jade ja o, K'elerekun jade ja o, A B'enu erekun sekete".

If the Challengers beat their opponents, then they would be singing thus – "A mo da won tan o, Eji perete L'oku, A mo da won tan o, Eji perete l'oku". But if they were beaten, they would be coming home one by one, without waiting for their companions. This will continue throughout the seven days.

As a strong royal mark of respect for the invaluable national work done by Moremi for the whole Ifes, it has from time immemorial been made a custom that as from the eve of the first day of celebration of Edi Festival, all the people in the palace must not make fire until about the mid day of the following day. Consequently, all the foods to be eaten in the palace throughout that day have to be brought by outside relatives of the people in the palace.

As a perpetual mark of royal punishment on the captured Igbos it has since the first celebration or Edi been made a continuous practice that the Igbos', (Now) generally known as Oluyares, or Igares, should be the makers of the fire which the palace people would use till the ensuing year.

It is not clearly known how this fire is actually yearly made; but it was in ancient days believed that it was made by means of some incantations uttered by the head of the Igbos; but the authenticity of this is not within our comprehension.

This ceremony is otherwise called "Isa Igare", because the Oluyares, otherwise called Igares, were reported to be the first to cook yams which the Ifes always call "Isa", when cut in pieces into pots on such a day.

The fire made on the first day of the Edi Festival usually lasts throughout the year, because it will be the eve of another year before the one for this year is put for another to be made the following day.

OMOLARERE DAY

On the second day of the ceremony, the authorities of the town will, as of old times, send some people to farm to fetch some tows which they will carry home in a covered up condition. This is called "Omolarere". It was, and still is, being used to represent the missing dead body of "Ela", already mentioned.

At first, when getting ready the tows to be carried home, people who went to fetch it used to say "E-di-i-dada" that is, tie it properly, as if it were really the corpse of Ela, just discovered. Consequently, what they yearly say tie properly like this, came to be known and called "Edi", that is, something bound up.

"Omo", as everybody knows, means, "child" in English. "Li", means where, or place. In Ife tongue, "Are, or A-a-re", means, on high; and hence, "Omo-li-a-a-re", now contracted to, "Omolarere", which means, here is the child we have been looking for on high, or the child we have been looking for on high is here, because when an Ife man says "Emi re", he means here am I; when he says "oun re," he means, here he is, or here it is, etc.

"Omo-la-re-re", was originally first said by the carriers of the assumed corpse of Ela, in order to show that his corpse was not missing, nor did he ascend to heaven as many people first thought until this day, this Omolarere, is annually carried home by the Ife-Ibadan Gate.

OWALARE DAY

As will be seen in the third part of this history, the name of "Owa" was derived from "He comes", which was the reply the Ooni used to get from his servants, bringing to him the annual tributes which the various other Obas used to bring to him in olden days.

Ilare is one of the five important quarters of Ile-Ife. It has from time immemorial been set aside for the annual show of everybody's best riches in wearing apparels; therefore, it was obligatory on all the societies of the town to go there in groups of well dressed people every year. The leader of each group and his lieutenants had to be carried shoulder high by the other members to and from this place. Many others of the remaining members of each society would be shouting "Lo-Ogun o", both in front and at the back on both journeys.

Before this date, each member of a society used to contribute money and seats for the success of the day. That day, is called "Owalare", which is a shortened form of "O-wa si Ilare", because every society in the town was in duty bound to put in its appearance at Ilare that day. As soon as a society arrived, its leader would send some of its younger members to go and greet the leaders of the other societies arriving before him. On the return of the messengers, the leaders who sent him would ask thus – "Does so and so society come?" In most cases the answer used, to be in affirmative, because any society which did not go to Ilare that day would not enjoy the recognition of the important people of the town.

Apart from the general decent dress of all sections on that day, Owalare was particularly used as the outing day for all the young women of the town having their first male children in life. In order to fit such women for that notable occasion all their well-to-do relatives and friends used, voluntarily to give them various costly wearing apparels. As no drum must be beaten during the Edi Festival until the evening of the last day of the whole celebration, those women as well as others had to dance to the music of the leather hand fans, called "Abebe", accompanied by palms of hands. They used to do this, up and down the long rows of many sitting societies until the fall of the day.

OJO IGBARUBI
(THE DAY OF CARRYING EVIL OUT OF TOWN)

The seventh day of the celebration of Edi Festival used, in olden days to be as interesting and enlivening as the first day was. That day was regarded as the one on which the corpse of Ela would be buried. Therefore, as the true adopted children of Moremi, everybody, except very old ones, used to make it a point of duty to witness the carrying away of the supposed corpse.

Unlike the Omolarere, carried home by a number of men from where the corpse of Ela was supposed to have been discovered, the supposed dead body to be buried is yearly carried till today, by only one minor chief, called "Tele". This Tele is known till today as the carrier of evil things out of town; and that is why the day he annually carries the supposed dead body of Ela out of town, for burial is called, "The day of carrying evil things out of town".

The position of this man was so dreadful that no son of the Ife soil has ever once been made Chief Tele, and it has from the very beginning been a title given to any chosen stranger in the town.

During the first six days, there must be no drumming of any kind throughout the town, although merriments of various types would be going on both day and night. The entire stoppage of drum is a sign that the whole populace were mourning for the death of Ela, who was made a scapegoat for the whole town. Therefore, the Ifes thought that during those six days, evil things of various types hanged on the whole town, and unless they were driven out of town, there would be no peace; and hence, the observation of the seventh day as the day of carrying evil things out of the town.

It is not really known to an average man in the street what the load which Tele yearly carries as the representative of Ela's corpse consists of, but everybody knows that the load is unusually wrapped up with palm leaves, and Omu or Imu leaves. Tele will dress himself with the same leaves and a piece of cloth round his waist.

Very long before the Tele comes out of a part of the palace where his load will be prepared and have himself properly dressed, the whole Erunwa Market and all its precincts, such as Oja'fe, Oke-mogun and Atiba, will be full to their utmost capacity of the people waiting to see Tele come out. As soon as he comes out, the whole people who have long been waiting for him will shout together "E-e-e-o, Moremi-Ajas'oro".

Tele will first of all go to Igbo Oja'fe, on the way leading to the town gate, through which the Igbos used to enter the town in times of old.

After offering a few words of prayer there, Tele and his huge crowd of followers will make a sharp right about turn, and direct their footsteps to the gate leading to Igbo'gbo, where the Igbos had been living on (now) Ife-Ondo road but formerly Ife-Ijebu road. The people following him will be singing thus – "O ngbedi, Tele ngbedi lo)". "He is carrying, Tele is carrying Edi away".

When Tele comes near to stream called "Omiokun", most of the people following him will disperse; leaving only a few with him. Tele will next turn left to a footpath leading to the grove, called "Igbo Ilamoja", used as Ela's grave. It is related that as soon as he turns to that side, he will begin to relieve himself of his heavy load by taking it off little by little, and throwing those small pieces into either side of the road until he reaches the marked place.

Although what he actually carries there is not known to an ordinary man, yet it is believed that the thing is capable of removing from Tele, all the bad things unanimously pronounced upon him by the whole towns people, and of putting them on anyone who will be so slow as to allow Tele to come out of that rove before him or her. Consequently, everyone or only a few, whose imperative duty it is to go into that grove with him always see to it that Tele does not leave them behind.

The other important people who also have to enter that grove that evening are – (1) a woman, whose chieftaincy title is Eri. She yearly goes there as the representative of Moremi, mother of the deceased, and (2) a man whose title is Yekere, the supposed man to bury Ela's corpse.

LEAVING THE GROVE OF ILAMAJA

When Yekere and Eri will be busily engaged in the performance of the final ceremonies in the grove, Tele will stand somewhere near them. As previously said, one of the tabooes attached to this part of the ceremonies is, that Tele must not come to the town before any of those people because it is believed that if he precedes any of them to the town, all the bad things pronounced on him will pile themselves on such a one.

Another taboo is the one which forbids Tele to come back home with the other people by the same way they all enter the grove. Therefore, when the other people will be coming back home by the way they have entered the grove, Tele will have to come back home by a newly made rough bush path. The purpose of this is that from very ancient times, it has been held a firm belief that if Tele reaches home before any of the people who entered the grove with him, that particular person will die before the round of the year.

Whether or not anyone has ever died as a real result of Tele's reaching home before him, it is not definitely known. Nevertheless, two things are known, and they are (1) Immediately after the ceremony, everybody usually makes it a point of duty to reach home before Tele. (2) The new road is believed to be yearly made in order to prevent Tele from reaching home before the other people.

ERI'S ANNUAL FREE GIFT

As Moremi, the mother of Ela, whose supposed corpse was as described above finally dealt with, was the principal person concerned in the first ceremony of the burial of her only son, she eventually regarded herself most unlucky person of all, upon whom a serious national misfortune had unrelentlessly so operated that she had to lose her only son. Therefore, she regarded it a necessity for her to waive away the seeming curse from her house.

Consequently, very early in the morning of the day following the "Igbarubi Day", Moremi woke up before anybody else in the town. Taking with her some articles already prescribed to her for waiving off the previously suspected curse in her house, with the one which was supposed might perhaps have befallen her in the grove in which she was with Tele, she went to the frequently used town gate to wash her head with a leg of an antelope, called "etu", which had been rubbed with a certain well prepared juju, capable of removing bad things from anybody, and carrying it to another person. There, she gave the meat to the first person who came out to see her.

As Eri yearly stands in place of Moremi, it has since

that time become an annual common practice for her to wake very early on the 8th day of the Edi Festival, to go with a leg of an etu, already medicated and go to a town gate, where she would give it to any person who would first come out to see her.

Although it was believed that any person who first see Eri on that day would die before the ensuing year, yet it has from time immemorial been tabooed that no one must refuse to receive that free gift of meat from her, so long as that person is the first to see her.

In order to avoid being an unfortunate victim of such a thing, everybody has since that time made it a point of duty, as far as possible to avoid coming in contact with Eri on that day. Nevertheless, it is believed that Eri has never failed to get somebody to give it to any year, because strangers who know nothing about this thing will not care to walk at any time of the day.

ODE-OMO OONI

As the members of all the ruling houses of Ife have two important things to do in connection with the celebration of the Edi Festival, every year, it is thought that the story of the Edi Festival will almost be incomplete without saying something about the two important parts annually played by the princes of Ife. The two things are – (1) Ode-Omo-Ooni, that is, Hunting period of the princes of Ife, and (2) Erukowo, that is, The feast which slaves are forbidden to witness.

This Ode-Omo-Ooni is yearly celebrated five days before the real Edi Celebration, under a certain tree, called "Ito", at Ilare quarter.

Ode-Omo-Ooni means a period when the whole members of the royal families of Ife yearly go a-hunting.

The celebration of this feast is as funny as it is

interesting. On that day, all the little holder Princes, called So-okos will stately dress themselves, and will be followed by their large followers carrying gourds, or demijohns of palmwine, bamboo wine, and other drinkables to Ilare. Here, the princes will enter a grassy place with cutlasses and sticks, looking for anything they can get to catch there. Sometimes they may not get any other thing than a lizard, or a grasshopper to kill; nevertheless, they will feel satisfied, so long as they can get something there to kill.

In the end, after drinks are finished, they all will dance back to the House of their leader named – "Wanikin".

ERU KO WO DAY

As a sign of deep sorrow for the lamentable fates of Moremi and her son, it has from time immemorial been arranged that Ooni should use that period as a hibernating one; and hence, when other people are dancing and eating about the town, Ooni and chiefs will keep in door. In order to compensate him for the period, the eighth day of the whole celebration is yearly set aside as Ooni's Feast Day for the whole of the titled Princes.

The So-oko title is so important to the Ife Princes that no one of them can become Ooni without first being a So-oko at least for seven days, if he did not bear the title before he is chosen to be an Ooni.

On that eighth day, Ooni usually shows his own share of the merriment of the Festival to the So-okos, the head of whom is "Wanikin". In order to show the superiority of the princes to the others who were in ancient days regarded as their salves, Ooni usually, makes a grand feast for the So-okos on this day. After the feast, both Ooni and the So-okos will dance to the entrance leading out of the palace to the Erunwa Market. At the gate, Ooni will go back, when the So-okos will be dancing out of the palace.

Those Whom Oduduwa Met At Ile-Ife

After it has been proved that the Igbos were not the actual people whom Oodua and his people met at Ile-Ife, the challenging and pertinent question which is naturally to be asked by every rational person is, "Whom did Oodua and his people met at Ile-Ife on their first arrival?

In these days of frequent and heated arguments, many people will not readily agree, if they are told that those whom the Ifes came to meet at Ile-Ife were not mere ordinary and visible living souls as we are. Nevertheless, they will be reminded that of all the idols worshipped in our whole country, the one called "Soponna" was, and yet is, the most dreaded. He is so much feared, that even today, no matter what your position in life may be, if you do not call him by his English name of "small pox", so long as you are a Yoruba man or woman, you can hardly call him by his real name "Soponna". As a mark of honour and respect for him, instead of calling him by his actual name "Soponna", from time immemorial, any of the following substituted names will be used – (1) Oba (King); (2) Obaluwaye (King terrestrial); (3) Olode (Owner of the Street); (4) Enire (The Good One).

Soponna was, and still is, so revered that if anybody is dead as a result of its attack, it must not be openly said that such a one is dead. It has long been a well established custom that in such a circumstance, instead of saying such a person is dead to say as follows – (a) The man has gone on a pleasure trip, (b) He has gone in company of the Good One, (c) He has joyfully strolled away.

Up till today, if anyone dies of it, no one must shed a single tear, and instead of sympathizing with the parents and relatives of the victim, the hearer of the sad news will say, "That's right, were I there, I would have helped the killer to kill the victim all the more". These are mainly said in order to avert Soponna's wrath from the hearer and his people.

From time immemorial, the firm belief of our people is that if anybody were to say openly that a person is dead of Soponna, numberless of people will eventually die of the same thing, because the saying so will tend to aggravate his wrath against everybody indiscriminately.

You may ask how they came about these horrible beliefs. These horrid general acceptances came to our whole people from the sad experience of the earliest Ifes after they had been unconsciously attacked by the "Eburus", who are the unseen soldiers of Soponna.

The epidemic so suddenly came upon the Ifes that within a very short period, a great number of them had died. As a result of this, they became so horror stricken that they went to consult Orunmila as to what the cause of their trouble was. In reply, Orunmila told them that in their night and very hot afternoon walks, they had come across some angry Eburus, who were the soldiers of Soponna, who was the king of this world. He said further that when Oodua and his people first came, Soponna moved his Eburus a little farther away for them; but as the Ifes were growing in number, they began to disturb the Eburus in their quiet unknown places to the Ifes.

When Oodua and his people heard this strange piece of intelligence, they decided to leave their first settlement. Consequently, Oodua and the majority of his people went to settle at "Oke-Ipao", now called "Oke-Owu". A part of them went to an adjacent place called "Iraye". Two other groups of them ran to settle on the way, now leading to Ilesa, and were subsequently known and called the Ido and Iloromu peoples respectively. Another group went by

Ilode Gate to go and settle at a place called Ile-Iwara till today.

When it remained only a few people, at Mo-ore, Obatala removed to Oke-Isokun, which is very close to Oke-Itase; and Orunmila himself removed to Oke-Itase, where he settled, just where the Ife Town Reservoir is today.

Feeling very much unhappy about this grave and unsatisfactory situation, Orunmila, who himself was a man of powerful and profound knowledge of mistery, started to find a way of easing the grave situation. Eventually, he detected a way of charming those unseen spirits so as to help the Ifes to live peacefully. It was from the charm (Ase or Ofo, or Ogede) which he then used against the unseen but powerful spirits that the name of the place in which he was then living was carved as "Oke-Ita-Ase" (now) contracted to "Oketase", meaning "Hill of Charming".

In course of time, Orunmila made a considerably substantial improvement in curbing the wicked activities of those invisible spirits. As many of the people who took refuge at Oke-Ipao, were not as happy in their new place as they were in their old place, they went to seek Orunmila's advice so as to know what they could do to enable them to come back to their old place with impunity. In reply, Orunmila said that they could not easily return without knowing how to deal with those unseen spirits. On further enquiry, from Orunmila, the latter said that the Ifes could combat the powers unseen if they were prepared to be his students in the art of studying secret things. Therefore, wishing to be free from their enemies, the Ifes started to study Ifa oracle, and the art of knowing charms and incantations. That is why all babalawo and the juju people, always refer to Ile-Ife as the birthplace of their arts.

The effectiveness of their studies has ever since earned

for the babalawos and the juju men the honour of being those to whom consultations should be made whenever anyone was attacked by an evil spirit, or whenever any person suddenly fell dead. At such a time, the babalawos and the juju men used to display their knowledge of incantations.

EFFECT OF THEIR EXODUS

This compulsory exodus of the Ifes to the various places already mentioned above had a very serious and indelible repercussion upon them all, because it eventually sharply divided them into two distinctive groups, now called "Ifes and Elus", as they are till even date known.

Those who went to "Oke-Ipao" being the first to return to the town, were, and are till today known as the Ifes. Those who went to Iraye or Oke-Awo, came back at a much latter time next to those of Oke-Ipao. Though their temporary King – "Oba-ni-Iraye" (now) abbreviated to Obalaye was not allowed to reign as an actual king on their return, yet, he was allowed to retain his title "Obalaye", as one of the high ranking Chiefs, with the title of "Elu". Though the others who did not return in time, were given the name of "Elus" as well, yet, their leaders were not allowed to enjoy the same privilege as Obalaye enjoyed, and still enjoys today, because they did not come back to town as Obalaye and his people did immediately after those of Oke-Ipao came back. At the time they came back, there was no more room for any senior chief again, and that is why they remain till today in the places of low ranking chiefs.

Going through this story, some people may think Ile-Ife more peculiar place than any other place in the world, in giving thought to the activities of the unseen spirits. In order that people may not be in darkness about this condition of life in other parts of the world, Saint Paul, that great Missionary among the heathens, made it pellucid in his Epistle to the Ephesians, Chapter 6, and verse 12, where it reads as follows — "For we wrestle not against flesh and blood, but against principalities, against powers, against the rulers of the darkness of this world, against spiritual wickedness in high places".

That the evil spirits can both move about, and talk is, transparently depicted in Saint Matthew's Gospel, the 8th Chapter, and 30th through 32nd verses reading thus — "And there was a good way off from them an herd of many swine feeding. So the devils besought him, saying, 'If thou cast us out, suffer us to go away into the herd of swine. And he said unto them, Go. And when they were come out they went into the herd of swine, and behold, the whole herd of swine ran violently down a steep place into the sea; and perished in the waters".

By these examples, it will be seen clearly that the ancient people who told the story that the people whom the Ifes met at Ile-Ife were no ordinary people, but spiritual and powerful ones, were not far from truth.

Index

www.ingramcontent.com/pod-product-compliance
Lightning Source LLC
Chambersburg PA
CBHW021904020426
42334CB00013B/479